THE DISRUPTER SERIES: ADVANCED ROBOTICS

HEARING

BEFORE THE

SUBCOMMITTEE ON COMMERCE, MANUFACTURING,
AND TRADE

OF THE

COMMITTEE ON ENERGY AND COMMERCE

HOUSE OF REPRESENTATIVES

ONE HUNDRED FOURTEENTH CONGRESS

SECOND SESSION

SEPTEMBER 14, 2016

Serial No. 114–169

Printed for the use of the Committee on Energy and Commerce

energycommerce.house.gov

U.S. GOVERNMENT PUBLISHING OFFICE

22–678 PDF   WASHINGTON : 2016

For sale by the Superintendent of Documents, U.S. Government Publishing Office
Internet: bookstore.gpo.gov   Phone: toll free (866) 512–1800; DC area (202) 512–1800
Fax: (202) 512–2104   Mail: Stop IDCC, Washington, DC 20402–0001

COMMITTEE ON ENERGY AND COMMERCE

FRED UPTON, Michigan
Chairman

JOE BARTON, Texas	FRANK PALLONE, JR., New Jersey
Chairman Emeritus	*Ranking Member*
JOHN SHIMKUS, Illinois	BOBBY L. RUSH, Illinois
JOSEPH R. PITTS, Pennsylvania	ANNA G. ESHOO, California
GREG WALDEN, Oregon	ELIOT L. ENGEL, New York
TIM MURPHY, Pennsylvania	GENE GREEN, Texas
MICHAEL C. BURGESS, Texas	DIANA DeGETTE, Colorado
MARSHA BLACKBURN, Tennessee	LOIS CAPPS, California
Vice Chairman	MICHAEL F. DOYLE, Pennsylvania
STEVE SCALISE, Louisiana	JANICE D. SCHAKOWSKY, Illinois
ROBERT E. LATTA, Ohio	G.K. BUTTERFIELD, North Carolina
CATHY McMORRIS RODGERS, Washington	DORIS O. MATSUI, California
GREGG HARPER, Mississippi	KATHY CASTOR, Florida
LEONARD LANCE, New Jersey	JOHN P. SARBANES, Maryland
BRETT GUTHRIE, Kentucky	JERRY McNERNEY, California
PETE OLSON, Texas	PETER WELCH, Vermont
DAVID B. McKINLEY, West Virginia	BEN RAY LUJAN, New Mexico
MIKE POMPEO, Kansas	PAUL TONKO, New York
ADAM KINZINGER, Illinois	JOHN A. YARMUTH, Kentucky
H. MORGAN GRIFFITH, Virginia	YVETTE D. CLARKE, New York
GUS M. BILIRAKIS, Florida	DAVID LOEBSACK, Iowa
BILL JOHNSON, Ohio	KURT SCHRADER, Oregon
BILLY LONG, Missouri	JOSEPH P. KENNEDY, III, Massachusetts
RENEE L. ELLMERS, North Carolina	TONY CARDENAS, California
LARRY BUCSHON, Indiana	
BILL FLORES, Texas	
SUSAN W. BROOKS, Indiana	
MARKWAYNE MULLIN, Oklahoma	
RICHARD HUDSON, North Carolina	
CHRIS COLLINS, New York	
KEVIN CRAMER, North Dakota	

SUBCOMMITTEE ON COMMERCE, MANUFACTURING, AND TRADE

MICHAEL C. BURGESS, Texas
Chairman

LEONARD LANCE, New Jersey	JANICE D. SCHAKOWSKY, Illinois
Vice Chairman	*Ranking Member*
MARSHA BLACKBURN, Tennessee	YVETTE D. CLARKE, New York
GREGG HARPER, Mississippi	JOSEPH P. KENNEDY, III, Massachusetts
BRETT GUTHRIE, Kentucky	TONY CARDENAS, California
PETE OLSON, Texas	BOBBY L. RUSH, Illinois
MIKE POMPEO, Kansas	G.K. BUTTERFIELD, North Carolina
ADAM KINZINGER, Illinois	PETER WELCH, Vermont
GUS M. BILIRAKIS, Florida	FRANK PALLONE, JR., New Jersey *(ex officio)*
SUSAN W. BROOKS, Indiana	
MARKWAYNE MULLIN, Oklahoma	
FRED UPTON, Michigan *(ex officio)*	

C O N T E N T S

THE DISRUPTER SERIES: ADVANCED ROBOTICS

WEDNESDAY, SEPTEMBER 14, 2016

House of Representatives,
Subcommittee on Commerce, Manufacturing, and
Trade,
Committee on Energy and Commerce,
Washington, DC.

The subcommittee met, pursuant to call, at 10:40 a.m., in Room 2322 of the Rayburn House Office Building, Hon. Michael C. Burgess (chairman of the subcommittee) presiding.

Members present: Representatives Burgess, Lance, Blackburn, Harper, Guthrie, Olson, Bilirakis, Brooks, Upton (ex officio), Schakowsky, and Kennedy.

Staff present: Gary Andres, Staff Director; James Decker, Policy Coordinator, Commerce, Manufacturing, and Trade; Graham Dufault, Counsel, Commerce, Manufacturing, and Trade; Blair Ellis, Digital Coordinator/Press Secretary; Melissa Froelich, Counsel, Commerce, Manufacturing, and Trade; Giulia Giannangeli, Legislative Clerk, Commerce, Manufacturing, and Trade, Environment and the Economy; Paul Nagle, Chief Counsel, Commerce, Manufacturing, and Trade; Mark Ratner, Policy Advisor to the Chairman; Olivia Trusty, Professional Staff Member, Commerce, Manufacturing, and Trade; Michelle Ash, Democratic Chief Counsel, Commerce, Manufacturing, and Trade; Lisa Goldman, Democratic Counsel, Commerce, Manufacturing, and Trade; Caroline Paris-Behr, Democratic Policy Analyst; Matt Schumacher, Democratic Press Assistant.

Mr. BURGESS. Very well. The Subcommittee on Commerce, Manufacturing, and Trade will now come to order. The Chair recognizes himself for 5 minutes for the purpose of an opening statement, and good morning and welcome to our witnesses.

OPENING STATEMENT OF HON. MICHAEL C. BURGESS, A REPRESENTATIVE IN CONGRESS FROM THE STATE OF TEXAS

Welcome to our hearing on advanced robotics, technology that has made its way into the United States in a variety of sectors.

This is the latest installment in our Disrupter Series covering technologies that are redefining our lives and improving our economic condition. It is 2016, and so many people my age will, of course, remember the cartoon "The Jetsons" and coming home to Rosie the Robot, who always had George Jetson's stuff all aligned for him, and many of us ask ourselves, "Where is Rosie the Robot today?"

Well, maybe today we are going to learn if we are not perhaps a little bit closer. But we are living in a world where you can actually use your iPhone to ask Siri, Alexa, or Cortana any question and get a real-time, accurate, and perhaps whimsical response.

Already advanced robotics are integrated into our economy with increasingly complex application, from manufacturing floors to surgical suites to fashion shows, as we learned from the lead on Drudge this morning.

Smart prosthetics are changing the lives of amputees and the elderly. Even some technologies that we have explored in previous Disrupter Series hearings leverage advanced robotic technology including the Internet of things and drones.

I look forward to hearing from our panel of witnesses about the real-world advanced robotics applications that students, academics, and industry professionals are all working toward.

Each of our witnesses today can give us a different view on the emerging trends and challenges presented by advanced robotics and technology.

The future workforce trends are particularly interesting. If it is true that more jobs will include some automation component in the coming decades, understanding how our students and professionals of all ages are able to acquire the skills necessary to adapt to this changing landscape is important to us as policy makers.

As with any new technology, it is critical to examine the benefits of the technology in weighing important consumer protection questions. Throughout our history, Americans have adopted and adjusted to economic shifts presented by new technology.

In our examination of these issues, it will be important to understand how consumers and businesses will be using the technologies and how they will be protected while preserving the flexibility and ingenuity of innovators that are driving this market forward.

Again, I want to thank our witnesses for taking the time to inform us about the exciting applications and the future potential benefits of advanced robotics.

[The prepared statement of Mr. Burgess follows:]

PREPARED STATEMENT OF HON. MICHAEL C. BURGESS

Good morning and welcome to our hearing examining advanced robotics—technology that has made its way into the U.S. economy in a variety of sectors. Advanced robotics' are integrated into our economy with increasingly complex applications, from manufacturing floors to surgical suites.

This is the latest installment of our subcommittees' Disrupter Series covering a variety of innovative technologies that are redefining our lives and improving our economic condition.

It is 2016, and we are not yet living in a Jetsons' world where Rosie the Robot greets you when you get home. However, we are living in a world where you can ask Siri, Alexa, or Cortana any question and get a real-time, accurate, perhaps whimsical, response.

Smart prosthetics are changing the lives of amputees and the elderly. Even some technologies that we have explored in previous Disrupter Series hearings leverage advanced robotic technology including the Internet of Things and drones.

I look forward to hearing from our panel of witnesses about the real world advanced robotics applications that students, academics, and industry professionals are working toward. Each of the witnesses here today can give us a different view of the emerging trends and challenges presented by advanced robotics technology. The future workforce trends are particularly interesting. If it is true that more jobs will include some automation component in the coming decades, understanding how are students and professionals of all ages able to acquire the skills necessary to adapt to this changing landscape is important.

As with any new technology, it is critical to examine the benefits of the technology and weigh important consumer protection questions. Throughout our history, Americans have adopted and adjusted to economic shifts presented by new technology.

In our examination of these issues, it will be important to understand how consumers and businesses using these technologies will be protected while preserving the flexibility and ingenuity of innovators that are driving this market forward.

I thank the witnesses for taking the time to inform us about the applications and future potential of advanced robotics. I look forward to a thoughtful and engaging discussion.

Mr. BURGESS. So we look forward to a thoughtful and engaged discussion, and I would like to yield the rest of the time to the gentlelady from Tennessee, Mrs. Blackburn, vice chairman of the full committee.

Mrs. BLACKBURN. Thank you, Mr. Chairman.

I do want to welcome our witnesses. I had the opportunity to meet Mr. Kamen a few months ago and talk with him about what he is doing in the field of robotics and the importance of that specifically to my district in Tennessee.

Brentwood Academy, which is in my district, the Iron Eagles are the international champions. They're putting an emphasis on robotics, and not only is it BA, but Vanderbilt University is developing some robotic devices for utilization of children with autism.

We are seeing other schools in the area begin to integrate robotics and the utilization of robotics, the development of this technology into core curriculums in science and math—the STEM activities.

It is a wonderfully exciting avenue for our students. I think it's so appropriate that we have this hearing that we look at this as a part of the Disrupter Series and not be fearful of it but engage what it is going to bring to productivity in the manufacturing marketplace, to our communities, to everyday tasks.

I talked with a couple of my fast-food franchise owners about the utilization of robotics in mechanization in the fast-food industry. Fascinating, the opportunities that it opens.

It does mean that we have to put an emphasis on the education so that we have a workforce that is excited about working in this area.

And Mr. Chairman, I will yield the time back to you or to whomever would like it.

Mr. BURGESS. The Chair thanks the gentlelady. The gentlelady yields back, and the Chair recognizes the subcommittee ranking member, Ms. Schakowsky, for 5 minutes for an opening statement, please.

OPENING STATEMENT OF HON. JANICE D. SCHAKOWSKY, A REPRESENTATIVE IN CONGRESS FROM THE STATE OF ILLINOIS

Ms. SCHAKOWSKY. Thank you, Mr. Chairman.

Today we are continuing our Disrupter Series with a hearing on advanced robotics. Robots are becoming increasingly sophisticated and at the same time robot technology is becoming cheap enough that people can actually bring robots into our homes, whether we are talking toys—that's been for a long time—but vacuum cleaners or other consumer products.

The potential for robotics is really great, and I'm interested in how we can help develop that potential. In June, I met with four girls from Mount Prospect, Illinois, who were part of a robotics team through Girl Scouts. They were in DC for the Global Innovation Challenge sponsored by the U.S. Patent Office.

If we want to continue in advanced technology then we certainly need to provide young girls and boys opportunities in science and technology.

FIRST Robotics has been a leader in encouraging students to pursue robotics, and I look forward to hearing more about that organization's work and from Mr. Kamen.

Some of the most innovative work in robotics comes out of our major research universities. For instance, Northwestern, which is in my hometown of Evanston, Illinois, has been collaborating with the Rehabilitation Institute of Chicago to research bio-inspired robotics.

They look at how fish swim and how the human hand moves and how animals use their whiskers and then use it to build robotics that can really improve the lives of persons with disabilities.

This research has tremendous promise, particularly for improving health care. Robotics also has significant implications for Federal policy. We need to invest in research and education that continues the technological progress that we see.

And as Mr. Burnstein and Dr. Kota note in their written testimony, robotics has changed the nature of American manufacturing.

We need to make sure that today's workers are prepared for this transition and that we are training today's workers for tomorrow's manufacturing jobs—or, really, today's manufacturing jobs.

As robotics become more commonplace in daily life we have to consider the implication for consumer safety and privacy.

Robots often collect and respond to information in their surroundings. How is that information used and how is it stored, who has access to that information, what does the consumer need to know, and when does the consumer provide consent?

These are questions that designers and consumer watchdogs must grapple with, and the answer may not be the same for all technologies. Robotics also raises questions of ethics and responsibility.

Let's say an accident occurs. This is a very real concern when we are talking about self-driving cars, for example. When does the fault rest with the manufacturer, when does it reside with the user?

Dr. Jones mentions several of these issues in her written testimony, and I look forward to hearing more from her on ways our Government can respond to this technological innovation. Dr. Jones defines robots as technologies that sense, think, and act.

Congress is not robotic, but I hope we will do the same thing in our subcommittee: Take the information, process that information, and then take action based on what we've learned.

I look forward to hearing from our witnesses and to working with my colleagues to ensure that Federal policy keeps pace with technological change. And I thank you, Mr. Chairman, and yes, I will yield to my colleague, Mr. Kennedy.

Mr. KENNEDY. I thank my colleague, Ms. Schakowsky.

I want to thank the chairman for calling this hearing and for continuing this series. Really interested in that prospect of and the testimony from our experts today.

Clearly, the opportunities for innovation around advanced robotics are almost limitless, and so I think, from my perspective, anyway, trying to understand how Congress can continue to support that innovation and support that progress is critical.

It does potentially bring up some interesting ethical questions and profound questions about the economic impact and questions about data and privacy and, potentially, jobs and the economy as well.

And Dr. Jones, you touched on that in your written testimony. So I'd like to start to explore just the broad base of those concepts and any guidance that you all might be willing to lend to us as innovations in this field continue to unfold at a pace that actually far exceeds, I think, that experts even a couple months or years ago. We are making tremendous progress in fields of advanced robotics, artificial intelligence, and others and what does that really mean, given the fact that we are moving more quickly than people even expected?

So with that, I yield back and I thank the chairman.

Mr. BURGESS. Chair thanks the gentleman. Gentleman yields back.

Chair recognizes the chairman of the full committee, Mr. Upton, 5 minutes for an opening statement, please.

OPENING STATEMENT OF HON. FRED UPTON, A REPRESENTATIVE IN CONGRESS FROM THE STATE OF MICHIGAN

Mr. UPTON. Thank you, Mr. Chairman.

So today our Disrupter Series turns to advanced robotics, for what I know will be an interesting and thoughtful discussion. I'm particularly excited to welcome my good friend, Dean Kamen, back to the committee. He has appeared a good number of times, adding his valuable insight to our 21st Century Cures effort, and, for those who don't know, he's often referred to as the Dean of Invention and has been at the forefront of disruptive technologies his entire career.

His decades of leadership and imagination have undoubtedly changed the face of advanced robotics from the invention of the Segway and iBOT electric chair to the drug infusion pump and so many others. His inventions and entrepreneurial spirit have led to the growth of the FIRST competition. FIRST, of course, stands for For Inspiration and Recognition of Science and Technology. His passion for innovation inspires kids from kindergarten to high school and encourages them to get involved in engineering and other STEM fields.

The program has grown from 20 teams to over 45,000 teams nationwide since it was founded in '89. I've got a great relationship with FIRST Robotics—very proud supporter.

My home State of Michigan is becoming Robot Central, with by far the highest number of FIRST teams per capita in the country.

To describe what this competition is like, FIRST teams receive a box with 120 pounds of components. They've got six weeks to design and build a functioning robot, and what they come up with in those six weeks is nothing short of amazing.

I've been to a number of competitions across the State, and I was impressed with what the kids are coming up with. It's inspiring. I want to stay there all day.

From the St. Joe Average Joes—this team—to the 2767 Stryke Force team in Kalamazoo, innovative STEM programs like FIRST allows for kids in our communities to dream big and inspire to become inventors, engineers, small business owners, community leaders. It's also refreshing to see kids excited by science, and I would note that Dean was treated like he was Bruce Springsteen walking into St. Joe High School, a rock star, for sure.

I'm also proud to co-sponsor bipartisan legislation with my colleague, Debbie Dingell, that would use the sale of commemorative coins for astronaut Christa McAuliffe, who was, of course, tragically lost in the Challenger disaster, to raise money for FIRST around the country, and I look forward to hearing even more from Dean and all of our witnesses about their recent efforts, whether it be FIRST, how Government had gotten involved with the program, and I also note that the Robotics Industries Association is headquartered in Ann Arbor—go, Blue.

Dr. Kota, among his many projects is a professor at the University of Michigan. Understanding how industry approaches advances in robotic technology, whether in capital investments or new partnership opportunities, is so critical to understanding how we move disruptive inventions from the lab into commerce to create jobs and economic growth here at home and a better quality of life for all.

I thank Chairman Burgess for continuing the series.

[The prepared statement of Mr. Upton follows:]

PREPARED STATEMENT OF HON. FRED UPTON

Today our Disrupter Series turns to advanced robotics for what I am sure will be an interesting and thoughtful discussion. I am particularly excited to welcome my friend Dean Kamen back to the committee. He has appeared a number of times, adding his valuable insight to our 21st Century Cures effort. For those who don't know, he's often referred to as the "Dean of Invention" and has been at the forefront of disruptive technologies his entire career. His decades of leadership and imagination have undoubtedly changed the face of advanced robotics. From the invention of the Segway and the iBot electric wheelchair to the drug infusion pump.

His inventions and entrepreneurial spirit have led to the growth of the FIRST competition. FIRST stands for "For Inspiration and Recognition of Science and Technology." His passion for innovation inspires students from kindergarten to high school and encourages them to get involved in engineering and other STEM fields. The program has grown from 20 teams to over 45,000 teams nationwide since it was founded in 1989.

I have a personal relationship with FIRST Robotics and am a very proud supporter. My home State of Michigan is becoming "Robot Central" with, by far, the highest number of FIRST teams per capita in the Nation. To describe what this competition is like: FIRST teams receive a box with 120 pounds of components and have six weeks to design and build a functioning robot. What they come up with in those six weeks is nothing short of amazing. I've been to numerous competitions across the State, and I'm always impressed with what the kids come up with. It's inspiring, it really is.

From the St. Joseph "Average Joes" team to the "2767 Stryke Force" team in Kalamazoo, innovative STEM programs—like FIRST Robotics—allows for kids in our communities to dream big and aspire to become inventors, engineers, small business owners, and community leaders. It is also refreshing to see kids excited by science, and I would note Dean was greeted like one of the Beatles when he visited St. Joseph High School back in my hometown.

I'm also proud to co-sponsor bipartisan legislation with my colleague Debbie Dingell that would use the sale of a commemorative coin for astronaut Christa McAuliffe, who was tragically lost in the Challenger disaster, to raise money for FIRST programs around the country.

I look forward to hearing even more from Mr. Kamen and all our witnesses about his recent efforts with the FIRST competition and how industry and the Government have grown involved with this program. I would also note that the Robotic Industries Association is headquartered in Ann Arbor and Dr. Kota, among his many projects, is a professor at the University of Michigan.

Understanding how industry approaches advancements in robotic technology, whether in capital investments or new partnership opportunities, is critical to understanding how we move disruptive inventions from the lab into commerce to create jobs and economic growth here at home.

I thank Chairman Burgess for continuing the Disrupter Series and highlighting the positive impact that emerging technologies, like advanced robotics, are having on our economy.

Mr. UPTON. I yield the balance of my time to my friend from Mississippi, Dr. Harper.

Mr. HARPER. Thanks for the high degree. So just no doctor—well, Doctor of Jurisprudence. Does that count?

Mr. UPTON. Yes, it does.

Mr. HARPER. OK. Thanks. Thank you, Mr. Chairman, for calling this hearing today, and I'm excited to continue this subcommittee's work on the Disrupter Series and looking forward to our discussion on advanced robotics.

In my district, Mississippi State University is actively conducting research and making advances through a number of projects in the robotics arena, including a National Science Foundation award to develop the Therabot, a therapeutic robotic support system in the form of a beagle dog that is responsive to touch through multiple sensors.

The Therabot will be used for therapy sessions with the clinician as well as for home therapy exercises, especially for individuals with post-traumatic stress disorder. Another project that's been funded in the past by Army Research Laboratories focuses on improving the integration of robots into law enforcement SWAT teams to develop new tactics and investigates how robots can be used more effectively in a real-world scenario to increase safety and information-gathering capabilities.

And those are just two of the many projects that are going on at Mississippi State. Additionally, at Mississippi State University they work with a number of organizations, including 4-H, to put together opportunities and competitions for students of all ages to learn about robotics and have some fun along the way.

With that said, I would like to welcome all the witnesses here today, in particular Mr. Kamen. It is good to hear from you and to have you be here and to explain these things to us and know how clearly committed you are to teaching children around the country technology skills that will prepare them for a bright future.

With that, I yield back.

Mr. BURGESS. Gentleman yields back. The Chair thanks the gentleman.

Seeing no other Members seeking an opening statement, we will conclude with Member opening statements. The Chair would like to remind Members that pursuant to committee rules, all Members' opening statements will be made part of the record.

And we do want to thank all of our witnesses for being with us here today, taking the time to prepare and to testify to the subcommittee.

Today's witnesses will have the opportunity to give an opening statement followed, of course, by questions from the Members. Our panel for today's hearing will include Mr. Dean Kamen, founder of DEKA Research; Dr. Sridhar Kota, Herrick Professor of Engineering at the University of Michigan; Dr. Meg Jones, assistant professor of Communication, Culture and Technology at Georgetown University; and Mr. Jeff Burnstein, president at Robotics Industries Association.

We appreciate you all being here today, and we will begin the panel with you, Mr. Kamen, and you are recognized for 5 minutes for an opening statement, please.

STATEMENTS OF DEAN KAMEN, FOUNDER, DEKA RESEARCH; SRIDHAR KOTA, PH.D., HERRICK PROFESSOR OF ENGINEERING, UNIVERSITY OF MICHIGAN; MEG LETA JONES, PH.D., ASSISTANT PROFESSOR, COMMUNICATION, CULTURE, AND TECHNOLOGY, GEORGETOWN UNIVERSITY; AND JEFF BURNSTEIN, PRESIDENT, ROBOTICS INDUSTRIES ASSOCIATION

STATEMENT OF DEAN KAMEN

Mr. KAMEN. Thank you. So I was told I have only a few minutes, and I decided, since a picture is worth a thousand words and a video is worth a thousand pictures, I took two videos. Trust me, they are each under 2 minutes long. One is sort of a general overview of FIRST, and it ties everybody together because it's the voice of God. It's Morgan Freeman from Mississippi, who, after coming, agreed to help us with the video because people trust the voice of God, and also said he will help us put FIRST in every school in Mississippi.

So we need to talk. We work with, of course, in Chicago RIC. My day job is medical stuff and robotics, and we built the arms that they are using for their optic stuff there and, of course, we work with Texas in many ways, Massachusetts.

You heard about how tired we are. But I'm going to show two videos. One is an overview of why robotics are going to be so valuable to the next generation and to this country in preparing to be competitive in the world.

The second one is a minute long, and it's not the voice of God. It's a 7-year-old girl that helped prepare a video for the international version of FIRST because we are seeing, for instance, incredible growth in 86 countries.

So another reason that you need to get serious about giving kids the skills they get through robotics is it's—and you'll see in that second video, "it's not robots, it's not robots"—it's all the skill sets for the 21st century, and I hope you listen to the 7-year-old. Let's hear from the voice of God.

[Video is played.]

So there's the voice of God. Now we go to a 7-year-old who's going to shake up the world with FIRST.

[Video is played.]

Mr. UPTON. Mr. Chairman, if I might just ask that—Dean, if we can—is it OK if we put that on the committee's Web site?

Mr. KAMEN. I would be proud to have you put it there.

Mr. UPTON. It's there. All right. Thank you.

[The prepared statement of Mr. Kamen follows:]

The Subcommittee on Commerce, Manufacturing, and Trade

Wednesday, September 14, 2016 at 10:30 a.m.

Disruptor Series: Advanced Robotics

Written Statement of Dean Kamen's Proposed Testimony

- I will describe the history of the non-profit I founded named *FIRST* (For Inspiration and Recognition of Science and Technology). I will also describe its mission and how it has evolved over the past 25+ years.
- *FIRST* is directly related to the "pipeline of talent" for robotics technology. I will explain how *FIRST* and its corporate sponsors are helping to fill that pipeline.
- *FIRST* uses robotics as a vehicle to introduce students to all the basic disciplines of science, technology, engineering and math and to give students an appreciation of these principles and tools.

Mr. BURGESS. Thank you, Chairman. Dr. Kota, you're recognized for 5 minutes for your opening statement, please.

STATEMENT OF SRIDHAR KOTA

Dr. KOTA. Chairman Burgess, Ranking Member Schakowsky, distinguished subcommittee members, thank you for the opportunity to appear before you today to discuss issues of critical importance to American economic competitiveness—robotics, artificial intelligence, and manufacturing.

My name is Sridhar Kota. I'm the Herrick Professor of Engineering at the University of Michigan and also the director for a new think tank called MForesight, the Alliance for Manufacturing Foresight.

MForesight works to bring together Government, industry, and research institutions to scan the horizon for emerging trends and promising opportunities for American manufacturing.

We help to build public-private partnerships related to manufacturing innovation. We respond to long-range technical questions from Government and industry and we work to identify best practices for training the next-generation workforce.

Our ultimate aim is to enable the United States to gain a long-term edge in economic competitiveness by strengthening domestic manufacturing.

Thirty years ago when I was a graduate student in mechanical engineering, robotics was already a topic on everybody's mind, but back then the dominant vision of robotics was of machines replacing human labor, taking over manufacturing tasks like welding and painting.

Today, researchers and firms tend to think of robots in a different light as collaborative tools to enhance productivity of factory workers, as a means to assist soldiers on dangerous missions, as co-drivers to enhance automobile safety and efficiency, and as co-inspectors to enable continuous monitoring and maintenance of high-value assets, such as bridges and wind turbines.

As artificial intelligence matures, there is promise that intelligent machines can augment certain types of human decision-making in fields ranging from medicine to manufacturing.

In short, robotics is now about augmenting and improving human work rather than replacing it. While robotics and AI innovations hold incredible promise, it's an open question whether the resulting technology products will be manufactured in the United States.

Despite Federal annual investment of over $140 billion in science and technology, America's trade deficits in advanced technology products moved from a surplus in 2001 to a deficit of over $90 billion in 2015.

To strengthen America's competitiveness in the age of advanced robotics and AI, we need to build the knowledge, skills, and infrastructure to anchor production here. Put concisely, we need to be thinking about translational research and workforce training.

I would first like to discuss translational research: how Government and industry can ensure that existing investments in basic research turn into useful new products, including robots and AI technologies, that create wealth for Americans and advance our national interests.

What I believe we need right now is a whole-of-Government approach that leverages the strength and missions of different Federal science and technology agencies to help ensure that we can translate promising discoveries and inventions into successful manufactured products.

This need not be costly. A national innovation foundation could be created by consolidating relevant offices at a dozen or more existing agencies.

Such an entity could be tasked with identifying the most promising basic research being undertaken across the Government and building public-private partnerships to invest in transforming that research into American-made products. The idea would be to maximize the return on taxpayers' investments in R and D.

The second policy matter I would like to discuss is education workforce training: how Federal, State, and local governments, working with employers, can ensure that Americans have the requisite knowledge and skills to build great products in the age of advanced robotics and AI.

In spite of our manufacturing losses in recent decades, there are now a large number of open positions in manufacturing and about 415,000 unfilled manufacturing jobs in the United States, according to the Society of Manufacturing Engineers.

I believe the biggest long-term risk to U.S. manufacturing isn't foreign competition. It's too little awareness and interest in engineering and manufacturing careers starting at an early age.

While high schools commonly require students to dissect a frog, few require students to disassemble a power tool, let alone a robot. This needs to change.

Primarily, the programs like FIRST Robotics—we all just saw those wonderful videos—it's an innovative program that challenges students to work together to build game-playing robots in an atmosphere of professionalism, and it is the roadmap to   engineering.

It is the roadmap to innovation, and right now it's currently done as an after-hour, after-school extracurricular activity.

This is the kind of program that we need to bring into the mainstream in order to mainstream curricula in K through 12, and that's the only way we can build a foundation for that next generation of innovation in the advanced manufacturing community.

So through smart research investments and sustained focus on education and training programs like FIRST Robotics, we can help ensure that these innovations truly improve American lives and livelihoods.

Thank you.

[The prepared statement of Dr. Kota follows:]

12 September 2016

Dr. Sridhar Kota's testimony

Chairman Burgess, Ranking Member Schakowsky, distinguished Subcommittee Members—thank you for the opportunity to appear before you today to discuss issues of critical importance to American economic competitiveness: robotics, artificial intelligence, and manufacturing.

My name is Sridhar Kota, and I serve as the Herrick Professor of Engineering at the University of Michigan. I also serve as the director of a new think tank called MForesight: The Alliance for Manufacturing Foresight. MForesight works to bring together government, industry, and research institutions to scan the horizon for emerging trends and promising opportunities for American manufacturing. We help to build public-private partnerships related to manufacturing innovation, we respond to long-range technical questions from government and industry, and we work to identify best practices for training the next generation workforce. Our ultimate aim is to enable the US to gain a long-term edge in economic competitiveness by strengthening domestic manufacturing.

Thirty years ago, when I was a graduate student in mechanical engineering, robotics was already a topic on everyone's mind. But, back then, the dominant vision of robotics was of machines replacing human labor— taking over manufacturing tasks like welding and painting. Today, researchers and firms tend to think of robots in a different light: as collaborative tools to enhance the productivity of factory workers, as means to assist soldiers on dangerous missions, as co-drivers to enhance automobile safety and efficiency, and as co-inspectors to enable continuous monitoring and maintenance of high value assets such as bridges and wind turbines. As artificial intelligence matures, there's promise that intelligent machines can augment certain types of human decision-making in fields ranging from medicine to manufacturing.

In short, robotics is now about augmenting and improving human work rather than replacing it.

While robotics and AI innovations hold incredible promise, it's an open question whether the resulting technology products will be *manufactured* in the United States. Despite federal annual investment of over $140 billion in S&T, America's trade deficits in advanced technology products moved from a surplus in 2001 to a deficit of approximately $90 billion in 2015.

To strengthen America's competitiveness in the age of advanced robotics and AI, we need to build the knowledge, skills, and infrastructure to anchor production here.

Put concisely, we need to be thinking about *translational research* and *workforce training*.

I'd first like to discuss translational research: how government and industry can ensure that existing investments in basic research turn into useful new products—including robots and AI technologies—that create wealth for Americans and advance our national interests.

What I believe we need right now is a whole-of-government approach that leverages the strengths and missions of different federal science and technology agencies to help ensure that we can *translate* promising discoveries and inventions into successful manufactured products. This need not be costly. A "National Innovation Foundation" could be created by consolidating relevant offices at 12 or more existing agencies. Such an entity could be tasked with identifying the most promising basic research being undertaken across the government and building public-private partnerships to invest in transforming that research into new American-made products. The idea would be to maximize the return on taxpayer's investments in R&D.

The second policy matter I would like to discuss is education and workforce training: how federal, state, and local governments—working with the employers—can ensure that Americans have the requisite knowledge and skills to build great products in the age of advanced robotics and AI.

In spite of our manufacturing losses in recent decades, there are now large numbers of open positions in manufacturing: as of April, there were about 415,000 unfilled manufacturing jobs in the United States according to SME. I believe the biggest long-term risk to U.S. manufacturing isn't foreign competition. It's too little awareness and interest in manufacturing careers, starting at an early age.

While high schools commonly require students to dissect a frog, few require students to disassemble a power tool—let alone a robot. This needs to change. Through programs like FIRST Robotics—an innovative program that challenges students to work together to build game-playing robots in an atmosphere of professionalism—we can give K-12 students meaningful first-hand experience in advanced manufacturing. By integrating such programming into curricula, enabling students to visit factories and meet workers, and restoring shop-class programming geared toward STEM learning and practical problem-solving, we can lay the foundation for an advanced manufacturing economy.

There's naturally uncertainty around the implications of robotics and AI. But it's up to us to ensure that their development is managed responsibly. Through smart research investments and sustained focus on education and training, we can help ensure that these innovations truly improve American lives and livelihoods.

Mr. BURGESS. Chair thanks the gentleman.

The Chair recognizes Dr. Jones, 5 minutes for your opening statement, please.

STATEMENT OF MEG LETA JONES

Dr. JONES. Chairman Burgess, Ranking Member Schakowsky, and distinguished members of the subcommittee, thank you very much for putting on this Disrupter Series and for inviting me to testify before you today.

With all of the excitement that comes with these ingenious advancements in robotics are ethical, policy, and legal questions.

Robot ethics and robotics policy conjure problems like how we avoid creating our mechanical overlords and when AI should have rights. These are questions for the future.

But what I'm going to talk about today is a really, really simple problem, and that is that robots don't have screens, and this is incredibly disruptive to privacy protection in the United States.

For the last 50 years, screens have been how we interacted with our information and communication technologies.

You engage with the cloud or a colleague or a retailer through the interface on your desktop, your laptop and then your smart phone and your tablet, and then for the last 20 years the Internet age has used that screen to create, collect, process, trade, and use your data, and it's through that same screen that you can figure out how your data is collected and used. You go to the bottom of the page and you click on the blue link that says privacy policy. And this is the notice and choice regime that information ex- change around the world had been built upon and the idea, of course, is that the data controller notifies you what they are going to do with your data, and you can choose to engage with the system or not.

There are, of course, problems with relying on this form of consent in the information age. People can't dedicate all of the time it would take to read all of those policies. Even if they could, they can't necessarily understand them, and even if they could read and understand them they wouldn't necessarily be able to assess the future uses and harms of their information.

Participating in one's data is increasingly difficult as screens get smaller, and we have seen this with smart phones and wearables already. But robots often don't have any screen at all.

Some robots are categorized within the Internet of things, and, as you are aware from previous hearings, the Internet of things is a catch-all for the movement to connect everyday objects to make them smart using sensors, wi-fi, and the cloud.

Like most technologies in the Internet of things, there is no screen, so if you want to know the terms of use for the privacy policy you can't scroll down on anything.

So how does one figure out what information is being collected and used, and why?

There was a 2015 Federal Trade Commission report on this subject, and they suggested using video tutorials, setup wizards, and privacy dashboards.

Treating the Internet of things like an extension of the Internet, these are tools that provide notice and participation for the good old days of personal computers and apps.

At Georgetown, we bought a bunch of Hello Barbies to figure out how we would know what she was collecting about us and what she did with the information just by interacting with her.

Now, to set up Hello Barbie, you have to click a bunch of accept buttons, like most things, but we really wanted to know what she would tell us.

So we asked her a number of times if she could keep a secret, or we would tell her something and then we would say, You're not going to share that with anyone, are you? And she couldn't really process the questions that we were asking her.

But when you asked her about her privacy policy, she said that an adult could find details about privacy on Page 2 of the booklet that came in the box.

So this is essentially the same problems that exist with relying on notice and choice in the Internet age, except you have the extra step that you have to go find this booklet or the box.

More importantly, what if it's not your Barbie? We are moving beyond the days of personal computers with smart objects, smart people, and smart environments.

When you get into someone else's driverless car or you see a drone flying overhead or you walk into someone else's smart office, what information is being collected?

How would you know? Whose drone is that? What company makes it? Do they collect information? Do they map your face for facial recognition? Where is the booklet that came in the box?

And even if you did know the answer to those questions, what can you really do about it? Notice and choice, even beyond the practical problems, breaks down at a theoretical level in what I call the Internet of other people's things, of which many robots will be a part.

So I know some people think that privacy is dead, and in my written testimony I noted a few statistics. But one of them is that, in January 2016, more American adults were worried about their privacy than losing their main source of income.

So people care, and I think that if we want to usher in the type of advanced robotics that we want, we have to start by innovating some of our policy approaches, including privacy.

Thank you.

[The prepared statement of Dr. Jones follows:]

PREPARED STATEMENT OF PROFESSOR MEG LETA JONES

For the

COMMITTEE ON ENERGY AND COMMERCE OF THE U.S. HOUSE OF

REPRESENTATIVES,

SUBCOMMITTEE ON COMMERCE, MANUFACTURING, AND TRADE

On

THE DISRUPTER SERIES:

ADVANCED ROBOTICS

Meg Leta Jones, JD, PhD

Assistant Professor of International Technology Policy

Communication, Culture, & Technology

Science, Technology, & International Affairs

Georgetown University

August 14, 2016

Prepared Statement of Professor Meg Leta Jones

Chairman Burgess, Ranking Member Schakowsky, and distinguished members of the subcommittee, thank you very much for initiating the Disrupters Series and for giving me the opportunity to testify today on some of the ethical and policy issues surrounding advanced robotics.

I am a professor of international technology policy at Georgetown University working in the Communication, Culture, & Technology program and an affiliate faculty member of the Science, Technology, & International Affairs program and the law school's Center on Privacy and Technology. The views I am expressing here today are my own.

"Robotics" is a broad term that encompasses many technologies and relates to even more. You are no doubt already familiar with some of the ethical and policy issues that arise from robotics. Many of them have been introduced in other sessions of the Disrupter Series, particularly those on drones, wearables, apps, and 3D printing. These include maintaining or improving privacy, security, prosperity, dignity, transparency, accountability, and efficiency across society.

Robotics shares many of these challenges, but all ethical issues are not shared by all robotic systems. For instance, driverless cars does not have the exact same problems as drones or caregiving robots. I will highlight one aspect of advanced robotics that is relevant to robots as information machines: privacy. In my testimony, I make three points:

1) Robots present a tremendous opportunity to innovate privacy protection.

2) Robots present a range of pressing ethical and policy challenges today that require interdisciplinary attention.

3) The federal government can contribute research funding, alternative governance structures, and deliberative spaces to these issues.

Robot Innovation, Policy Innovation

Without a strict definition, robots can simply be described as the category of technologies that sense (take in information about the environment), think (process that information), and act (take some action in or on the physical environment).[1] Another popular conception of robots is a computer that can perform the job of a human, which includes those that are stationary, mobile, software, and hardware.[2] Robots are often part of other technology categories such as aircraft or motor vehicles. I will be discussing robots as technologies within the internet of things ("IoT"). IoT is the label that encompasses the movement to computerize and connect everything in our lives. Already everyday objects like thermostats, light bulbs, mattresses, pregnancy tests, refrigerators, and cars are internet-enabled. Many of these objects are robots.

Advancements in robotics and artificial intelligence brings along concerns about ethical design and use as well as policy considerations. "Robot ethics" and "robotics policy" conjure fascinating, complex questions like how to avoid creating robot overlords[3] or whether and when robots should be granted rights.[4] My remarks are confined to ethical and policy concerns arising today or in the near future from human interaction with robots. I will use my oral testimony time to speak about privacy issues and have included additional brief descriptions of other relevant topics and potential governance strategies in my written testimony.

---

[1] Ryan Calo, *Robotics and the Lessons of Cyberlaw*, 103 Calif. L. Rev. 513 (2015).
[2] "March of the Machines," 60 Minutes CBS News (Jan. 13, 2013).
[3] James Barrat, Our Final Invention: Artificial Intelligence and the End of the Human Era (2013); Nick Bostrom, Superintelligence: Paths, Dangers, Strategies (2014).
[4] Lawrence B. Solum, *Legal Personhood for Artificial Intelligences*, 70 North Carolina L. Rev. 1231 (1992); Kate Darling, *Extending Legal Protection to Social Robots: The Effects of Anthropomorphism, Empathy, and Violent Behavior Towards Robotic Objects*, in Robot Law (Ryan Calo, Michael Froomkin, and Ian Kerr, eds. 2016).

1. Robots and Privacy

Robots are information machines. They take in and crunch an extraordinary amount of data to function properly, optimize performance, and tailor experience. And they are poised to herald in a new wave of technological disruption. In 2007, Bill Gates observed, "The emergence of the robotics industry is developing in much the same way that computer business did 30 years ago."[5] Similar social, ethical, and legal challenges like security threats, alienation from the real world, alterations of cognitive workings, intellectual property disputes, deterioration of human relationships, and changes in the nature of work present themselves in the robotics context. Notable among these concerns is privacy. Those robots intended to interact with people will take in information about individuals, and some will collect, store, process, and share personally identifiable information to provide more tailored or optimized engagement – or simply because they can.

People care about privacy, even if their actions sometimes suggest otherwise.[6] In May 2015, Pew Research Center found that 93% of adults felt it was important to have control over *who* could get information about them and 90% felt it was important to have control over *what* information is collected about them.[7] In January 2016, a report from the TRUSTe/National Cyber Security Alliance (NCSA) Consumer Privacy Index revealed that more Americans are worried about their data privacy than about losing their main source of income.[8] So, in order to encourage

---

[5] Bill Gates "A Robot in Every Home," Scientific American (Feb. 1, 2008), http://www.scientificamerican.com/article/a-robot-in-every-home-2008-02/.

[6] Alessandro Acquisti and Jens Grossklags, *Privacy and Rationality in Individual Decision Making*, 2 IEEE Security & Privacy 24 (2005); Alessandro Acquisti1, Laura Brandimarte, and George Loewenstein, *Privacy and Human Behavior in the Information Age*, 347 Science 509 (2015).

[7] Mary Madden and Lee Rainie, "Americans' Views about Data Collection and Security," Pew Research Center (May 20, 2015), http://www.pewinternet.org/2015/05/20/americans-views-about-data-collection-and-security/.

[8] Brian Mastroianni, "Survey: More Americans Worried About Data Privacy than Income," CBS News (Jan. 28, 2016), http://www.cbsnews.com/news/truste-survey-more-americans-concerned-about-data-privacy-than-losing-income/.

the innovation and adoption of robotics, as well as actively participate in the creation of technologies that shape society on behalf of constituents, the opportunity to innovate policy approaches to privacy should be seized.

1.1 Notice and Choice

For at least the last fifty years in the Computer Age, notice and choice, as part of the Fair Information Practices Principles, has dominated the meaning and effectuation of privacy in U.S. policy. Notice and choice regimes are intended to notify users of information collected, processed, and used, then provide users with a choice of whether to engage with an information system; the regime establishes a form of informational consent. For the last twenty years in the Internet Age, if you wanted to know how a website or platform gathered and used your information, you could locate and read the privacy policy, usually found hyperlinked at the bottom of each page on a screen. Users can also navigate many online environments in privacy-preserving states using various settings like Google's incognito mode and are often provided and encouraged to revisit their privacy settings through dashboards on screens. These forms of user participation are often given as justification for limited regulations to protect privacy.

Problems with this regime have been uncovered and detailed by researchers since the early 2000s.[9] These include the inability of users to read[10] and understand[11] so many policies and whether a real choice[12] can be made. Participation is hampered by users' inability to know who will be given access to and potential uses of their information in the future, and retroactive

---

[9] Daniel Solove, *Privacy Self-Management and the Consent Dilemma*, 126 Harv. L. Rev. 1880 (2013).

[10] Aleecia M. McDonald and Lorrie Faith Cranor, *The Cost of Reading Privacy Policies*, 4 I/S: A Journal of Law and Policy for the Information Society 540 (2008), http://moritzlaw.osu.edu/students/groups/is/files/2012/02/Cranor_Formatted_Final.pdf.

[11] Helen Nissenbaum, *A Contextual Approach to Privacy Online*, 140 Daedalus 32 (Fall 2011), http://www.amacad.org/publications/daedalus/11_fall_nissenbaum.pdf.

[12] Kirsten Martin, *Transactions Costs, Privacy, and Trust: The Laudable Goals and Ultimate Failure of Notice and Choice to Respect Privacy Online*, 18 First Monday (2013) http://firstmonday.org/ojs/index.php/fm/article/view/4838/3802

correction or deletion is rarely provided as information moves from the original collector to other parties.[13] Today, apps and wearables add a layer of difficulty to notice and choice because it is simply hard to find and read the privacy policies on the devices.[14]

1.2 Privacy without Screens

In an age of smart objects, the Robotic Age, notice and choice breaks down almost fully. Screens, like those on your phone and computer, have formed the foundation of our experience with connected content and information exchanges and participation in the collection and use of our personal data. Robots don't have screens. And a lack of screens promises to further complicate the notice and choice arrangement.

The Federal Trade Commission's internet of things report advises designers and manufacturers of IoTs to protect privacy. The FTC report explains:

> Staff acknowledges the practical difficulty of providing choice when there is no
> consumer interface and recognizes that there is no one-size-fits-all approach. Some
> options include developing video tutorials, affixing QR codes on devices, and
> providing choices at point of sale, within set-up wizards, or in a privacy dashboard.
> Whatever approach a company decides to take, the privacy choices it offers should
> be clear and prominent, and not buried within lengthy documents.[15]

One can imagine opening up their new drone or robotic personal assistant and watching a video tutorial or clicking through a setup wizard making various selections about data collection and use. Smart objects include the same issues with participating in one's data online but adds an

---

[13] Meg Leta Jones, Ctrl+Z: The Right to be Forgotten (2016).
[14] Notice and choice *can* work effectively in many contexts to give people confidence and comfort in their information exchanges. *See* Ryan Calo, *Against Notice Skepticism in Privacy (and Elsewhere)*, 87 Notre Dame L. Rev. 1027 (2012).
[15] *Internet of Things: Privacy & Security in a Connected World*, FTC Staff Report (Jan. 27, 2015), available at https://www.ftc.gov/system/files/documents/reports/federal-trade-commissionstaff-report-november-2013-workshop-entitled-internet-things-privacy/150127iotrpt.pdf.

extra step because it requires the user to go find a screen. Take for instance Hello Barbie, Mattel's newest wifi-enabled smart toy that uses voice-recognition to allow kids to have a "real" conversation with Barbie. When one asks Barbie, who records every single interaction, about her privacy policy, she does not ask if you want her to keep your conversation for a certain amount of time or if there are some things she should keep a secret; instead, she explains that an adult can find details on page 2 of the manual that came in the box.[16]

1.3 The Internet of Other People's Things

The robotic future will not be filled with *your* robots and your robots alone. We will regularly interact with other people's robots. In a world where you get into a driverless Uber, walk into someone else's smart home, look up to see a couple drones flying overhead, or play with someone else's Hello Barbie, when and how are you to know what the information practices are and choose to avoid the system? Moving through a smart environment with robots working in various contexts does not present many opportunity to work through a setup wizard or watch a video tutorial. It does not present opportunity to participate in the use of your data.

Even if it did, it's not your robot. The information practices are selected by someone else. In fact, many elements of the Fair Information Practices Principles that relate to an individual's ability to control their information, including access to and correction of personal information, are very challenging, if not impossible, in a robotic environment. This is the problem of the Internet of Other People's Things.[17]

1.4 Innovating Privacy

While the FTC should be applauded for proactively considering IoT, an opportunity to invest in solving problems from the Internet Age is being missed. Robotics offers a moment to

---

[16] Meg Leta Jones, *Your New Best Frenemy: Hello Barbie and Privacy Without Screens*, 2 eSTS 242 (2016).
[17] Meg Leta Jones, *Privacy Without Screens and the Internet of Other People's Things*, 51 Idaho L. Rev. 639 (2015).

consider new concepts, new policies, new rules for new technology instead of treating IoT and robots as extensions of the internet. Even the opt-in versus opt-out debate is a stale in the Robotic Age. How can one opt-in or out of data collected by a robot barista or a coffee shop that uses a facial recognition assistant to improve service for regulars? The Robotic Age may be one of an ever-public wherein information is relentlessly collected and processed by unknown entities.[18] But, it does not have to be.

I suggest there are at least two alternative approaches to privacy. The first alternative is a set of legal standards similar to those enacted by the European Union in the Data Protection Regulation; the Article 29 Working Party has published a report outlining its approach to IoT and has a working group on robotics.[19] The second alternative retains notice and choice as central but reverses it. Individuals could notify robotic systems of their information choices and expect that those choices would be respected unless otherwise informed. You can think of this in terms of a robots.txt file -- used by web site operators to instruct web robots like search engine crawlers to *not* visit certain pages – for people. By working with roboticists, ethicists, and policy researchers, more ideas will emerge.

---

[18] Margot Kaminski, *Robots in the Home: What Will We Have to Agree To?*, 51 Idaho L. Rev. 661 (2015).
[19] Article 29 Data Protection Working Party, Opinion 8/2014 on Recent Developments on the Internet of Things (Sept. 16, 2014), http://ec.europa.eu/justice/data-protection/article-29/documentation/opinionrecommendation/files/2014/wp223_en.pdfs.

2. Other Ethical and Policy Issues of Note

A plethora of ethical and policy issues exist for today's robotics community. Below is a select set of these issues.[20]

2.1 Laws and Liability

It would be nice if robots could simply be programmed to obey the laws or follow a code of ethics, but that is much easier said than done. Laws are vague, difficult to interpret, challenging to translate into computer code, context specific,[21] and generally grant individuals the autonomy to break them if they choose.[22] Determining any ethical code presents similar challenges – should the designers, companies, policymakers, public,[23] or individual make the choices that dictate the actions of robots?[24]

Robotics as an industry faces legal uncertainty similar to that which faced personal computers and internet sites before it. For instance, Ryan Calo argues that in order to open up robotics to additional innovators – to turn robots into platforms that can be improved upon or altered for additional functions with third party or open-source software or physically adapted like personal computers and smart phones ("open robotics") – liability should be limited similarly to the way Section 230 of the Communications Decency Act immunizes platforms from liability arising from content posted by users on the platform.[25] Other liability issues exist

---

[20] Many of these problems have been presented at the We Robot Conference, an annual conference that brings together engineers, computer scientists, ethicists, social scientists, and law scholars to discuss robotics policy.
[21] Lisa Shay, Woodrow Hartzog, John Nelson, Dominic Larkin, and Gregory Conti, *Confronting Automated Law Enforcement*, in Robot Law (Ryan Calo, Michael Froomkin, and Ian Kerr, eds. 2016).
[22] Ian Kerr, *Digital Locks and the Automation of Virtue*, in From Radical Extremism to Balanced Copyright: Canadian Copyright and the Digital Agenda (Michael Geist, ed. 2010).
[23] "Why Self-Driving Cars Must be Programmed to Kill," MIT Technology Review (Oct. 22, 2015) (detailing early stages of the "Moral Machine" project, a kind of crowdsourcing for ethical determinations in the trolley problem available at moralmachine.mit.edu), https://www.technologyreview.com/s/542626/why-self-driving-cars-must-be-programmed-to-kill/.
[24] Jason Millar, "You Should Have a Say in Your Robot Car's Code of Ethics." Wired (Sep. 2, 2014).
[25] Ryan Calo, *Open Robotics*, 170 Maryland L. Rev. (2011); Ryan Calo, "The Need to Be Open: U.S. Laws Are Killing the Future of Robotics," Mashable (Jan. 1, 2014), http://mashable.com/2014/01/01/us-law-robotics-future/#XVDAU.9TKsqV.

in traditional settings such as healthcare facilities that may utilize robotics equipment in surgeries, pharmaceutical distribution, or expert diagnosis systems.[26] The opacity of robotic systems, the mix of numerous technologies from various sources, and complexity of human-machine interaction[27] complicates traditional notions of accountability.

2.2 Automated Decisions and Communication

Algorithms – the "thinking" portion of robotics – currently make decisions that impact our lives every day in highly controversial ways. They may be used to present news on Facebook, search results on Google, credit offers, job interviews, and stock prices.[28] How those processes can be "fair" and transparent is one aspect of the problem.[29] Whether, when, and how humans are and should be involved in these processes is another.[30] Algorithms, as communication producers, can also lie and demean. In 2012, Google repeatedly called Bettina Wulff, former first lady of Germany, a prostitute. When users typed "Bettina Wulff" into the search bar, Google – intending to be helpful – filled in the rest with suggestions based on the searches of other users. In this case the phrase "Bettina Wulff prostitute" emerged from Google's algorithm and was presented to users around the world in various languages.[31] In 2016, it took the Twittersphere less than a day to teach Microsoft's guileless AI chatbot @Tay, designed as an experiment in "conversational understanding," to be misogynistic, racist, and xenophobic, causing the company to pull her off the platform.[32] These are problems that derive from the

---

[26] Jason Millar and Ian Kerr, *Delegation, Relinquishment and Responsibility: The Prospect of Expert Robots*, in Robot Law (Ryan Calo, Michael Froomkin, and Ian Kerr, eds. 2016).

[27] Nicholas Carr, The Glass Cage: Automation and Us (2014).

[28] Frank Pasquale, The Blackbox Society: The Secret Algorithms That Control Money and Information (2015).

[29] Malte Ziewitz, ed., Governing Algorithms, 41 Special Issue of Science, Technology, and Human Values (2016).

[30] Meg Leta Jones, *A Right to a Human in the Loop*, SSRN Working Paper (2016), http://papers.ssrn.com/sol3/papers.cfm?abstract_id=2758160.

[31] Meg Leta Ambrose and Ben M. Ambrose, *When Robots Lie: A Comparison of Auto-Defamation Law*, IEEE Workshop on Advanced Robotics and its Social Impacts (2014);

[32] James Vincent, "Twitter taught Microsoft's AI Chatbot to be a Racist Asshole in Less than a Day," The Verge (Mar. 24, 2016), http://www.theverge.com/2016/3/24/11297050/tay-microsoft-chatbot-racist.

underlying data (and sometimes design oversight). No one at Google actually called Ms. Wulff a prostitute; instead its algorithms processed the information, data, and clicks input by users to present searchers with what they were probably looking for. Algorithms learn by being fed data by engineers and users. Smart technologies can thus exacerbate existing inequalities and stereotypes[33] and cause new types of informational harms and injustices.

2.3 Jobs and the Economy

For those that have lost their jobs to robots, they suffered what economist call technological unemployment,[34] one of the primary concerns surrounding automation in American policy throughout the 20th century.[35] The impact robots will have on the national and international economy and workforce is highly disputed. MIT economists Erik Brynjolfsson and Andrew McAfee argue that technological unemployment explains a recent jobless recovery and that while technology has always destroyed and created jobs, the pace of current technological replacement prevents the previous adaption made by human job creators and workers.[36] Other commentators disagree about the pace of displacement, the agility of workers, the eventual outcomes, and on what present attention should focus.[37]

---

[33] Kate Crawford, "Artificial Intelligence's White Guy Problem," NY Times (June 25, 2016); Zeynep Tufekci, "The Real Bias Built In at Facebook," NY Times (May 19, 2016).
[34] John Maynard Keynes, *Economic Possibilities for our Grandchildren*, in Essays in Persuasion (1972, originally published 1930).
[35] Thomas Rid, The Rise of the Machines: A Cybernetic History (2016).
[36] Erik Brynjolfsson and Andrew McAfee, The Second Machine Age: Work, Progress, and Prosperity in a Time of Brilliant Technologies (2014); Erik Brynjolfsson and Andrew McAfee, Race Against the Machine (2012).
[37] *See e.g.* Martin Ford, The Rise of the Robots: Technology and the Threat of a Jobless Future (2015) and Jerry Kaplan, Human's Need Not Apply: A Guide to Wealth and Work in the Age of Artificial Intelligence (2015).

3. What the Federal Government Can Do: Invest, Innovate, & Organize

Today, the answers to these ethical dilemmas matter less than how we answer them. An American approach to robotics should not interfere with but foster the establishment of human-robotic systems that promote trusted, reliable, transparent, and interactions,[38] that protect the dignity of not only those engaged with robotics but also those that are not.[39] To establish such an approach, the federal government can continue to invest in robotics broadly, innovate existing governance structures, and organize deliberative spaces.

3.1 Invest

Investing in robotics not only means funding improvements of sensors, algorithms, kinetics, or telecommunications. It also means supporting those investigating human robotic interaction, the sociology of robotic integration, the ethics of design, and new policy approaches. The National Robotics Initiative is a five-year-old, multi-agency effort among the National Science Foundation, NASA, the National Institutes for Health, the U.S. Department of Agriculture, the Department of Defense, and the Department of Energy to accelerate the development and integration of robots that work beside or cooperatively with people. NRI's call is expansive:

> Methods for the establishment and infusion of robotics in educational curricula and research to gain a better understanding of the long-term social, behavioral and economic implications of co-robots across all areas of human activity are important parts of this initiative. Collaboration between academic, industry, non-profit and other organizations is strongly encouraged to establish better linkages between fundamental science and technology development, deployment and use.

---

[38] David A. Mindell, Our Robots, Ourselves: Robotics and the Myth of Autonomy (2015).
[39] Sheila Jasanoff, The Ethics of Invention (2016).

These types of broad calls are welcome and will benefit the resolution of ethical and policy issues moving forward.

3.2 Innovate

As investments are made in the robotic future, bringing a broad array of perspectives to its formation is vital to ethical robotics. "The law cannot keep up with technology" is a well-established idiom but is not a necessary truth. Robotic innovations present an incredible opportunity to move many of the conversations relevant to law and policy from the end of technological integration to the conception, design, and implementation of technology. This may include experimenting with increased ethical training for roboticists,[40] embedding ethicists in robotics teams,[41] engaging with the broader public to find contemporary answers to ethical questions,[42] promoting diversity in robotics,[43] and/or creating ethical guidance or standards through working groups.[44]

3.3 Organize

Finally, the federal government can organize diverse, multidisciplinary deliberative spaces,[45] as well as events for public participation in the robot revolution. In January 2016, Ryan Calo and Dr. James Kuffner organized an incredible event entitled Policy for Autonomy Workshop, co-sponsored by the National Science Foundation and the Department of Homeland Security. Bringing together industry participants from the car, computing, and other

---

[40] Byron Newberry, *The Dilemma of Ethics in Engineering Education*, 10 Science and Engineering Ethics 343 (2004).

[41] A. van Gorp and S. van der Molen, *Parallel, Embedded or Just Part of the Team: Ethicists Cooperating Within a European Security Research Project*, 17 Science and Engineering Ethics 31 (2011).

[42] Sheila Jasanoff, *Technologies of Humility: Citizen Participation in Governing Science*, 41 Minerva 223 (2003).

[43] *See* Carnegie Mellon University's Girls of Steel Robotics initiative, http://www.frc.ri.cmu.edu/girlsofsteel/our-team/about-us/.

[44] Meg Leta Jones, *The Ironies of Automation Law: Tying Policy Knots with Fair Automation Practices Principles*, 18:1 Vanderbilt Journal of Entertainment & Technology Law 77 (2015).

[45] Sheila Jasanoff, The Ethics of Invention (2016).

technology sectors, ethicists and legal researchers, and university roboticists, the workshop represented a unique and exciting ongoing conversation. For two days, the group brought forward complicated policy problems, uncovered inconsistencies in language and concepts, and sought to identify similarities and differences among various contexts. Organizing these and other types of deliberative spaces, including events open to the public, is an important role for the federal government to play.

Thank you for your time and attention, and the opportunity to testify today. I would be pleased to answer your questions.

Mr. BURGESS. Chair thanks the gentlelady.

Mr. Burnstein, you are recognized for 5 minutes for your opening statement, please.

STATEMENT OF JEFF BURNSTEIN

Mr. BURNSTEIN. Thank you, Chairman Burgess, Chairman Upton, and Ranking Member Schakowsky and members of the subcommittee.

I want to really thank you for having the Robotics Industries Association here to participate in this series. RIA has been around since 1974, and we are based in Ann Arbor, Michigan—go, Blue—and what's interesting about RIA is that it represents 400 companies that are driving innovation, growth, and better, safer and higher-paying jobs in manufacturing service industries.

Now, I have been there for over 30 years, and I have to tell you this is the most exciting period for robotics and American innovation in robotics in the entire time I've been there.

We think that the key to staying competitive in manufacturing, in particular, is to implement advanced robotics. We see what's happening around the world. RIA is in China, we are in Korea, we are in Japan.

We see the efforts that are going on there and in Europe, and we think we have an opportunity here to create more jobs and to save jobs that are already here.

I'd like to, if you don't mind, highlight some of our member companies and the innovations they are working on. In the Boston area, Rethink Robotics is developing collaborative robots.

These are a new kind of robots that work side by side with people, that don't require safety fences between them. Or Soft Robotics, also in Boston, who's taken on a challenge that's kind of plagued the industry for many years of how to grip different parts. So you have very fragile things that have to be picked up by a robot, like produce or vegetables and tomatoes, peaches—all the things that agriculture cares about. You have these hard parts— rugged, on assembly lines. You used to have to change the gripper, the hand on the robot. But now, thanks to companies like Soft Robotics, you might be able to do it with just one gripper.

Aethon in Pittsburgh, Pennsylvania, creating an autonomous robot that delivers and tracks medical supplies in hospitals, allowing the staff to focus more time on patient care, which is really what we want.

And how does this all play out at user companies? When, there is a company we work closely with called Vickers Engineering in New Troy, Michigan, a precision machining company that provides solutions to automotive, oil and gas, agriculture, defense, and industrial markets.

They had trouble keeping people in dull, repetitive, and dangerous jobs. They had to keep hiring and retraining. It was hurting productivity. They said, Why don't we take a shot at robotics? And they did. Their business tripled, bought more robots and at the same time they increased their head count, and we are seeing this across the country with small and medium-sized companies as well as large ones.

One thing the U.S. is fortunate to have is the greatest group of system integrators in the world. Now who are these companies?

These are folks that put together the systems that actually make the robots work on the factory floor that integrate with the other machines and equipment and tie into the Internet of things.

Companies like Genesis Systems in Davenport, Iowa, and Matrix Design in South Elgin, Illinois, Schneider Packaging Equipment in Bremerton, New York, Tennessee Rand from Chattanooga, Tennessee. These are just a few of the certified robotic integrators that RIA would like to acknowledge.

Today's robots offer U.S. manufacturers improvements in efficiency that are driving profits and employment, as we said. We issued a white paper on this called "Robots Fuel the Next Wave of Productivity in Job Growth."

You may read otherwise, that robots are job killers, but our data doesn't support that. What we see is that whenever robot sales rise, unemployment falls. And when the opposite happens—when robot sales fall—unemployment rises. You don't hear that in the media too often.

We understand the importance of education, STEM education, and training and retraining to make sure that we've prepared our workforce for the future jobs and for the present jobs.

There are groups like RAMTEC in Marion, Ohio, a Government- and industry-supported collaboration that provides training to high school and college students along with incumbent workers to support industry's needs for training in robotics and automation equipment.

And we hope that programs like this will proliferate because by working together industry, Government, academia can help make sure that our workers are prepared for the future.

I personally appreciate this opportunity to highlight the important role that robotics is playing in advancing our economy in creating not only safer, better, and higher-paying jobs but also improving society and our health and our livelihood and our long-term ability to be productive members of society.

I hope that those of you who aren't involved will join the House Robotics Caucus with Congressman Rob Woodall and Congressman Mike Doyle, and we value their work and look forward to continuing the dialogue on advanced robotics.

Thank you very much.

[The prepared statement of Mr. Burnstein follows:]

Testimony to the House Energy and Commerce

Subcommittee Commerce, Manufacturing and Trade

Wednesday, September 14, 2016

Jeff Burnstein, President

Robotic Industries Association

Chairman Burgess, Chairman Upton, Ranking Member Schakowsky and Members of the Subcommittee,

Thank you for inviting me here today to participate in the Disrupter Series hearing on Advanced Robotics. I am Jeff Burnstein, President of the Robotic Industries Association, headquartered in Ann Arbor, Michigan. Our 400+ members drive innovation, growth, and safety in manufacturing and service industries through education, promotion, and advancement of robotics, including related automation technologies and integrated solutions.

Personally, I have been with the Robotic Industries Association for more than 33 years. According to many industry leaders in the late 1970s and early 1980s, robotics was going to be the next industrial revolution. In the mid-1980s, some wrote the robotics industry off as having failed since it didn't grow as quickly as predicted, and many U.S. companies exited the market such as IBM, General Electric, Westinghouse, and more. But, over time, with innovation and persistence, the robotics industry now offers technology and expertise from American companies that are disrupting industries all over the world. And, most importantly, robotics is saving and creating jobs as it helps develop the world in which we all have the opportunity to live longer, better, and more productive lives.

<u>Testimony</u>

Robotics has already changed the world, but more fundamental change is clearly ahead. It is much easier to see the outline of the eventual new world than to know how soon it will arrive.

We hear a lot these days about things like smart cities, smart mining, and smart farming. Let's remember that this all due to smart *people*. In the robotics industry, we take a perspective that goes beyond technology for technology's sake. We strive to understand the impact of our work on people's lives, and to make the world better instead of worse. This is an area where government has its own crucial perspective, and where partnership between industry and government is essential.

Together, we must embrace the reality that industry is driving change at an accelerating rate, and we can't slow this acceleration. It is driven by our human nature to positively disrupt and push the innovative boundaries. This passion for change leverages our competitive advantage to be the world-wide leader in the advancement of robotics, which will be key to the manufacturing revival in the Unites States. When companies improve their competitiveness through the implementation of advanced robotics, they are saving jobs and creating ripples of positive change and economic impact in their workplace and communities.

Advanced Robotics: Engaging Challenges in Every Industry

Behind every technological innovation is a human that identified a real-world problem worth solving. In a sense, robotics is less a standalone industry than a way of engaging challenges in every industry. In the history of the industrialized world, we have often asked people to perform work that is dirty, dangerous, repetitive, and ultimately unsatisfying. Robots allow people to use their brains, not their brawn and to perform this work more profitably and safely.

Included with the testimony is RIA's 20-year look at robots and the impact on jobs which shows that whenever robot sales rise, unemployment falls. Conversely, when robot sales fall, unemployment rises. This trend is visible in nearly every country where robot use is accelerating. This may seem counterintuitive, and is opposite of what is often portrayed in the media and by studies that fail to account for the job saving and creation that occurs because of robots.

Today, with advances in robotics and automation, companies are returning their manufacturing to the United States. A recent report by Boston Consulting Group states, "The share of executives saying that their companies are actively reshoring production increased by 9% since 2014 and by about 250% since 2012. This suggests that companies that were considering reshoring in the past three years are now taking action. By a two-to-one margin, executives said they believe that reshoring will help create U.S. jobs at their companies rather than lead to a net loss of jobs."

A great example of a company that has become more competitive through robotics is RIA member, Vickers Engineering of New Troy, Michigan. A medium-sized prototype and production supplier of CNC machining to automotive and other industries, Vickers had trouble finding and keeping people to do dull and repetitive jobs. They tried robotics and discovered that this saved the cost of constant hiring and retraining for positions people didn't want. Then, because of lower costs, improved productivity and greater product quality, they were able to win business that they couldn't win before. As a result, they hired more people than they had before they started using robotics.

This story is repeated at many small and medium sized companies throughout America, stories that we chronicle on our "Why I Automate" video series on the www.a3automate.org website. Another great example is Marlin Steel, a RIA member company from Baltimore, that determined they could no longer compete in the bagel basket industry since Chinese companies could make and ship similar products to the US for less than it cost Marlin to buy the steel. They implemented robots, increased productivity, and improved the quality of their baskets so much that they were able to hold higher value products than bagels. They began selling baskets at much higher prices to automotive, aerospace, and medical customers. Like Vickers Engineering, Marlin ended up with more people who were in safer, better, and higher paying jobs. Best of all, they began exporting their products to China.

Ironically, the robotics industry's biggest challenge today is finding good people to fill the open jobs they have in designing, building, installing, operating and maintaining robots. While many of the positions require engineering backgrounds, there are also many that only require two-year degrees from community colleges or certificates from technical schools. This is true for almost every one of our 400+ member companies.

Agriculture

Agriculture has always been fertile ground for technological innovation – from the cotton gin and mechanical threshers to tractors, hydraulic implement lifts, and genetically-modified seeds. As we learn to feed and clothe more people with a limited supply of land, labor, and money, we are under pressure to accelerate this innovation due to the obstacles faced in the agriculture workforce along with the world's growing demand for quality food supply.

Farming can also be dangerous business. Office of Safety Health Administration (OSHA), reports that human workers are at risk exposure to an array of hazards from livestock handling injuries to chemical and pesticide exposure.

Advanced robotics is providing the solutions for a more efficient, productive, and safer farming environment. Today, in the fields, drones are 3D mapping fields to identify crop stress or issues with equipment, creating digital elevation models, and supplying a level of insight previously available only by physically walking the land. Modern precision farmers are largely data driven, using GPS data and aerial surveys to assess crop yield and soil health in numerous field locations then creating "prescription maps" of exactly where to apply precise amounts of fertilizer, other chemicals, and even seed at exactly the right time. One example is Rowbot, through a partnership with Rowbot Systems LLC and Carnegie Robotics LLC., the autonomous robot travels between rows of corn and applies nitrogen fertilizer more precisely and at the optimum time in the growing cycle to improve crop yields.

The obstacles facing the agricultural labor industry also impact the harvest of delicate crops like peaches and tomatoes. RIA member, Soft Robotics from Cambridge, Massachusetts has built a new class of adaptive and inexpensive robotic grippers that can pick and handle delicate crops like peaches and tomatoes, supplementing human pickers and enabling higher yields.

Health Care

From surgical robots that can mill out precise fittings for a hip replacement to personal assistant robots that help care for patients, medical robots are transforming the face of healthcare. For an industry challenged by out of control costs, explosive amounts of information and technology, labor shortages, and an aging and increasingly sick population, advanced robotics can ease the labor gap and improve efficiency and safety to serve more patients with higher quality.

Robots in the operating room enable less invasive surgical techniques that improve patient care and reduce recovery time. In 2000, Intuitive Surgical's da Vinci Surgery System from broke new ground by becoming the first robotic surgery system approved by the U.S. Food and Drug Administration (FDA) for general laparoscopic surgery. The da Vinci system facilitates complex surgery with a minimally invasive approach, powered by robotic technology that allows the surgeon's hand movements to be translated into smaller, precise movements of tiny instruments inside the patient's body. Robot-assisted surgery, coupled with advances in telemedicine and faster internet, will enable surgeons to operate on a patient in another city, state, or even on another continent. The first long-distance telesurgery was performed successfully in 2001 between New York and Strasbourg, France.

The single-incision port is another robotic surgery innovation, where a doctor could make a tiny incision then, using an access port something like RIA member, Medtronic's SILS port, insert the snake-like arms of a robot through that incision. According to Dr. Michael Palese, a urological surgeon and the Director of Minimally Invasive Urology at Mount Sinai Hospital in New York City who specializes in robotic, laparoscopic, and endoscopic surgery, "The next generation of this technology will mean that you put one little hole in the patient and then put snake-like arms through that hole ... That would change the nature of surgery forever."

Outside the operating room, robots are supporting a more reliable and efficient pharmaceutical tracking distribution system. RIA member Aethon has developed a chain of custody system that tracks a medication from the initial order from the physician to the final distribution to the patient. The MedEx software solution secures and tracks medications in real time while giving the medical staff visibility into the status and delivery of the medication. Once the medication is ready for distribution, Aethon's TUG, an autonomous mobile robot, travels hallways, rides elevators, and navigates obstacles to deliver it to the nursing unit. This eliminates distractions for pharmacy staff and boosts accuracy and productivity, ability to track medication also allows pharmaceutical staff less distractions in their environment, rather than taking calls from staff, they are able focus on the accuracy of filling and distributing medications.

In RIA's Robots and Healthcare Saving Lives Together, Aethon reported that their software helped hospitals that typically receive 200 missing medication requests a day to reduce that number to 10. TUG also works 24/7 to transport goods, materials, and clinical supplies throughout the hospital. This means that staff can focus on patient interaction and assisting with nursing instead of dealing with logistics or pushing of heavy, clumsy carts throughout the hospital.

The benefits of automating a medical research lab include sifting through massive amounts of data in a short period of time. Scientists at a National Institutes of Health laboratory search for the right combinations of chemicals to fight diseases. Robots can test millions of potential drug combinations that would overwhelm human capabilities. Robots that are traditionally used in the manufacturing space can also be specially engineered to work in a clean laboratory environment. They handle plates with diseased cells and test against 450,000 different chemical combinations to find solutions. Not one of the tests is duplicated and this shows how automated equipment can learn to handle unique data.

Robotics equipment in labs can work without harm near biological contaminants, radioactive material, and toxic chemotherapy compounds. Companies in all industries handling hazardous materials can automate and make more strategic use of people and keep them safe.

Manufacturing

Manufacturers are adopting more automation than ever before. For many, it's no longer a question of whether to automate, only when and to what extent. With wages offshore rising, robot prices down, and performance up, robot sales are at an all all-time high. In August, RIA reported the first half 2016, a total of 14,583 robots valued at approximately $817 million were ordered from North American companies during the first half of 2016. The number of units ordered in the first six months marks a new record to begin the year, growing two percent over the same period in 2015, which held the previous record.

Automation changes the kinds of jobs that are available. A skills gap report by Deloitte says that, in the coming decade, there will be 3.4 million available automation jobs but only 1. 4 million qualified workers. To fill these jobs with qualified workers, we need deep partnership between industry and government. We need automation suppliers and users, colleges, technical and career centers, government, parents and teachers, mentors and volunteers – all working together.

Humans and robots working side-by-side leverage the best of both worlds. Collaborative robots are designed to work alongside employees to handle the repetitive and mundane tasks of picking and handling, while employees focus on the actions that require human judgment (e.g., fitting components). RIA member Rethink Robotics developed two lines of robots, *Sawyer* and *Baxter*, which are working side by side with employees of General Electric. At RIA's International Collaborative Robots Workshop, Roland Menassa, Global Research Automation Center Leader for GE Global Research in Van Buren Township, Michigan, said, "Sawyer was grabbing parts and putting them in the assembly. But the human was making sure it was fitting properly and inserting the last screws, using what humans are good at – dexterity, perception, and logic. For us, elevating the role of the human on the assembly line to focus on quality – to focus on the value-added – is very important."

Human-robot collaboration increases output, lowers costs, and produces a higher quality product. MIT researchers have found that robots collaborating efficiently can be more productive than teams made of either humans or robots alone, and reduced human idle time by 85 percent. Centers such as the Advanced Robotics Manufacturing Institute aims to work with industry, governments, and academia to develop and implement advanced robotics into the next generation of manufacturing facilities.

Robotic Systems Integration and Component Manufacturing

One thing that isn't well known about the robotics industry is that the robot arm itself is only one element of a successful robot system. The US is fortunate to have the world's most experienced and talented base of system integrators – the companies who build entire factory floor automation systems, in which the robot is just one component. Robot systems integration is the hub of all communication, coordination, purchasing, logistics, and planning in an automation project. The goal of the integrator is to provide a turnkey automation solution while optimizing efficiency, safety and quality. My own organization's RIA Certified Robot Integrator Program has gained recognition for providing robot integrators with a way to benchmark against industry best practices while at the same time allowing robot users to develop a baseline for evaluating robot integrators.

Many robotic systems integrators are enjoying great business success, creating new jobs across the US. One RIA member, Genesis Systems in Davenport, Iowa, has performed over 4,500 robotic system installations and integrated 5,535 robots in the automotive, aerospace, and light and heavy industrial markets. Genesis has work cells located in 42 states and 15 countries. Another RIA member, Matrix

Design in South Eglin, Illinois, reported that incoming orders for the first half of 2016 increased significantly compared to the prior year. As a result, Matrix has expanded its operations in South Eglin and opened a new office in Indianapolis.

System integrators, in turn, rely on manufacturers of robotic system components. These manufacturers provide highly innovative parts for robotics systems, such as tool changers, machine vision systems, and robotic accessories. They are expanding, growing jobs, and supporting their local economies through the expansion of the use or robotics.

For example, RIA member ATI Industrial Automation from Apex, North Carolina, manufactures robotic accessories and products that can be found in thousands of applications. ATI has grown its workforce from 5 to over 200 employees, while supporting commercial, government and university partners in advancing robotic solutions.

One growing area in robotic system components is machine vision, which serves as a robot's eyes. For example, RIA member Cognex Corporation of Natick, Massachusetts produces machine vision systems that are used in factories, warehouses and distributions centers around the world to guide, inspect, identify and assure the quality of items during the manufacturing and distribution process.

Overall Impact on Jobs and the Economy

From the many examples presented above, we see that robotics is an opportunity to innovate, not just with technology, but the types of jobs that are available. This is just a stage in a continuing process – technology has been changing the nature of jobs for hundreds of years. For example, a small fraction of the population work on farms today compared to the beginning of the century, but we now produce more food that can be processed and distributed more quickly and safely, and farm workers have new jobs that more closely meet the current generation's lifestyle choices. Similarly, jobs as horse and buggy drivers, elevator operators, and gas station attendants (in most states) have largely gone away, thanks to technology.

But even in this era of exploding technological advances that has seen record shipments of robots in the U.S. and around the world, U.S. employment has continued to rise, along with improvements in labor productivity. (See the Association for Advancing Automation's (A3) report Robots Fuel the Next Wave of U.S. Productivity and Job Growth.) Over the years, predictors, have typically overestimated the ability of technology to replace human beings. It's been half a century since Rosie, the Jetson's maid, first appeared, but the closest we've come to a successful home robot is a vacuum cleaner.

In many cases, robots are used for the dull and dangerous jobs that today's workers simply don't want. Coupled with changing demographics and the graying of the manufacturing workforce, automation is ideally suited for many of the roles for which companies struggle to find workers.

Advancement of robotics and other automation often creates highly desirable new jobs. For example, the Deloitte report mentioned earlier posits that the next decade will see 3.4 million manufacturing jobs with only 1. 4 million qualified workers to fill them. We saw that, in many situations, robots augment and collaborate with human workers rather than replace them: robots do the heavy lifting while human workers program and monitor the process, applying their unique skills in new positions. At the same time, labor costs in emerging markets continue to rise, eroding the cost advantages of offshore manufacturing. As companies bring operations back to the U.S., they are often using robotics to help them remain cost-competitive in global markets by increasing product output, quality, and consistency.

When companies improve their competitiveness through automation, saving jobs in the process, they also create ripples of economic impact—and jobs—in their communities. If factories are shuttered, neighborhoods are destroyed. But when manufacturers instead maintain or regain competitiveness by automating effectively, they are able to grow their own businesses and also support other jobs in the community, including supplier companies, restaurants, stores, hospitals, schools, and other services that support local factory workers.

There is one critical area where we are seeing a robotics-related job crisis. The robotic industry's number one problem today is there aren't enough qualified people to design, program, install, operate, and maintain robots. Good, high-paying jobs are waiting for people with the right training, which can often be acquired at technical schools and community colleges. Companies need educated machine operators with basic skills in robot programming, integration, and maintenance, as well as specific expertise such as machine vision applications. This expertise must be built through science, technology, engineering, and math (STEM) programs in K-12, vocational and technical programs in robotics that are reinforced through industry-academia partnerships, as well as higher education programs in specific engineering fields.

A recent RIA article "Closing the Skills Gap in Automation: A Call for Action" identifies the importance of strong education and industry partnerships to support the current and future skills needed for the advancement of automation. An example, Robotics Advanced Manufacturing Technical Education Collaborative (RAMTEC), partnered with Yaskawa, FANUC, Honda, Lincoln Electric, and RobotWorx, to operate an industrial robotics and advanced manufacturing training center, located in Marion, Ohio.

RAMTEC provides training to high schoolers and college students, along with incumbent workers to support industry's need for training on robotics and automation equipment.

In 2014, PEW Research asked nearly 2,000 prominent technology experts to respond to a question on the economic impact of robotic advances and artificial intelligence. More than half (52 percent) believe technology will not displace more jobs than it creates over the next ten years. According to the PEW report AI, Robotics, and the Future of Jobs, these experts "have faith that human ingenuity will create new jobs, industries, and ways to make a living, just as it has been doing since the dawn of the Industrial Revolution."

Respondents on both sides of the debate share concerns that our educational institutions are not adequately preparing workers for the skills that will be needed in the job market of the future. Industry and government must work together to solve this problem. I appreciate the opportunity to be here with you today as one step toward this shared goal.

Mr. BURGESS. The Chair thanks the gentleman, and the Chair would note that Mr. Doyle is a member of the full committee of Energy and Commerce.

So I thank you all for your testimony, and we'll move now into the question and answer part of the hearing.

Mr. Burnstein, let me just ask you, because in your written testimony you referenced using robotics to do jobs that perhaps would be inherently too dangerous for a person to do—a hazmat situation. We're all familiar with the bomb-disabling robots that several of our police departments used in Dallas, Texas, this July—July 7th. So kind of a unique situation where there was a shooter who had killed several Dallas police officers and an officer with the Dallas Area Rapid Transit, and the individual was contained in a garage but could not be controlled, and ultimately Chief Brown made what I consider a very courageous, a kind of unique, decision to use the bomb-disabling robot to actually deliver a bomb to this individual and end the problem.

I am sure, from your association, are you aware of that instance?

Mr. BURNSTEIN. Yes, I am.

Mr. BURGESS. Are there thoughts that the association has on the use of the robot in that situation? Again, I think Chief Brown was courageous, and I am grateful that he made the decision. I'm grateful he prevented any further loss of life. But, obviously, it poses some new questions.

Mr. BURNSTEIN. It does pose new questions and, I think, ideally, robots wouldn't be involved in harming people. It's one of the first laws of robotics that Isaac Asimov laid out.

However, in this particular case, if you take the word robot out of the equation, we sent in equipment that would save police officers' lives. And so whether it was a robot or some other way to get that in there, if we could have got a person in there we would have taken that shooter out in that way.

So, in my opinion, that was the right choice and it was a good use of the technology because it was saving police officers' lives.

Mr. BURGESS. Very good, and I appreciate your answer.

So, Dean Kamen, earlier this week the One Hundred Year Study on Artificial Intelligence released a report titled "Artificial Intelligence and Life in 2030."

So the good news: The panel found that there is no cause for concern that artificial intelligence is an imminent threat to humankind or the United States Congress. Actually, I just added that.

In fact, the findings of the group of academics from the University of Texas at Austin, MIT, Harvard, and others concluded that increasingly useful applications of artificial intelligence with potentially profound positive impacts on society and the economy were likely to emerge between now and 2030.

So, simply, do you agree with their assessment? You spend a lot of time in this space.

Mr. KAMEN. Well, I think that the whole term artificial intelligence, or for that matter robotics, means different things to people, let's say, within that industry and to the public.

I would almost define robotics as seen by the public as any piece of technology that wasn't around when you were a kid because the fact is we've been robotically doing more and more and more since

the industrial revolution started, and before that, you know, knit-
ting machines made things robotic, and artificial intelligence, a machine that is programmed to do a function—the calculator you have
was considered, you know, a mathematician 30 or 40 or 50 years
ago.

I think we should always be concerned, as you heard from Dr.
Jones about unintended consequences, of applying technology to
anything, but artificial intelligence, like most good tools, will just
support the real stuff, and we could all use a little more of the real
intelligence.

And I think as long as humans with good judgment and good
ethics are deploying these tools for the betterment of the world, we
are OK. It would be naive to assume that you can never do damage
with it.

But, again, the first tool—the rock—could help you build a house
or break your thumb. That first use of fire could make us have a
life and could burn down your house. Every new technology bears
the potential to be misused.

But putting your head in the sand is just going to allow somebody else to dominate that technology, and I'd rather be the ones
that decide how to develop it and how to use it.

Mr. BURGESS. Thank you. You know, my background is in health
care. I think some of your work has been in the healthcare space
and, of course, we are all familiar now with robotics in the operating room. Could you speak to that just a little bit, what the future might hold for us?

Mr. KAMEN. So you mentioned in your opening remarks Rosie,
and I think, again, the word robot, coming originally from the
world of science fiction, always displays the robot as this
anthropomorphic thing,

I think of all the things that robots will evolve to, the least likely
is that, because we are pretty good at being what we are.

We like being what we are, and we are not going spend a lot of
time and money making something else to do what we are and
what we like to do. You're not going to build a robot to take your
trip to Disney.

I think robots will be used like other technologies that are developed, to augment, as you heard from Dr. Kota, what we do. There
will be robots much bigger than us, like bulldozers. We don't like
digging ditches. There will be robots much smaller than us, ones
that will travel through your vascular system, go in there and
tweak that heart valve so you don't need to have it removed or re-
placed.

Robots will get very small. Robots will get very big. Robots will
not look like humans. But in the healthcare field, they will change
so dramatically the process of taking care of people that a doctor
50 years from today will not recognize, and certainly a hospital will
not look like it looks today.

Nanotechnology, proteomics, genomics, the ability to use robotic
technology to get to critical places without destroying vital tissue,
it's going to change virtually every concept we've had in medicine
more than you've seen medicine change so far in your lifetime.

Mr. BURGESS. And it has changed a lot, even in my short lifetime.

Chair thanks the gentleman for his answers. The Chair recognizes Ms. Schakowsky, 5 minutes for your questions, please.

Ms. SCHAKOWSKY. Thank you, all of you. It's been a fascinating panel and really excellent testimony.

I wanted to ask you, Dr. Jones, a couple of questions. In all our exuberance, I'm happy that you raised some issues that we, you know, also need to pay attention to: privacy and data security.

Robots, almost by definition, collect a vast amount of information because they need to sense the environment they are in and process the information and take action based on that information. And as you pointed out in your testimony, many robots are or will be Internet connected.

And at the subcommittee's hearing on wearable devices, we heard about notice and choice like those you mentioned earlier. We generally rely on screens to provide the interface that allows for notice and choice, but, as with wearables, robots generally don't have those screens.

So let me also say for household robots that are already on the market, let me ask you, What is the mechanism used to provide notice to consumers and, is it always a question of the privacy policies are just included in the box, you better take them out and save them?

Dr. JONES. Yes, for the most part. When you buy a device for your home, you're still at least within the Internet of things, not other people's things.

And so when you put a nest system, for instance, in your home, you click a number of boxes and you can find out more information about what's collected. And sometimes you have to, just to set the thing up. And so there is sometimes increased amount of notice in the Internet of things.

However, if you walk into someone else's house that has, say, a personal assistant robot that wires the home and does voice recognition or facial recognition, you don't have a way to express to that system, hey, I don't like that, don't do that to me, I don't want you to map my face and store it somewhere. And I think that that is really the next hurdle, and it's a wonderful interdisciplinary problem.

It requires a lot of technical considerations as well as policy and ethical considerations. I don't think that it's necessarily a regulatory change.

That being said, I do think that reliance on notice and choice will have to take a secondary seat to something.

Ms. SCHAKOWSKY. You know, at one of these hearings I brought a privacy policy that was included in the box and kind of unfurled it. It was very long. It was very legalistic. Very small print. Challenging.

But you also mentioned that, online, how many people—let's be honest—read all the words before they push "agree," because you know that you're not going to get in unless you agree.

And so, you know, I think these are challenges that we need to figure out. But let me ask you this—you mentioned a study by the Pew Research Center that found that a vast majority of adults felt it was important to have control over what information was collected about them and who could get that information.

49

And do you agree that most consumers would prefer a more customizable approach?

Dr. JONES. So this, I don't know, there are a lot of surveys on privacy, and I think that they are not tailored to regulatory answers a lot of the time.

So you'll hear people say they really care about privacy. But it's not clear whether they want a set standard like the European version of privacy or they want an adjusted type of notice and choice, a more sort of libertarian privacy integrated into the way they engage with ICTs.

So I can't say for sure. I think that Americans probably don't care. They just want privacy.

Ms. SCHAKOWSKY. OK. When legislators discuss privacy and data security issues, some have argued that we should only be concerned about a narrow set of data of personal information, specifically personal financial information.

However, consumers have more than financial concerns, and I'm just wondering if you could discuss the privacy concerns that robots have beyond the financial, and how do we broaden the discussion to ensure we understand the emerging technologies and the privacy concerns that come with those new technologies?

Dr. JONES. So, for anyone who cares about their physical safety, a robot could easily be something to be concerned about because, if a robot registers that you're near them, for instance, someone could know where you're at.

We have seen a number of apps that have shown the location of women, for instance, that have been not held positively by Congress or the public at large, but physical location data is one thing. The idea that you can figure out a lot of things about someone that they don't want you to know by putting together a few pieces of information, we know that that is also true. So right now we have a ton of little pieces of information that gets put together that can show basically your route to work, where you work, what you do, where you go to lunch, who you go to lunch with, and by put- ting sensors in the environment, you just increase that dossier on every individual that's moving through those spaces.

And what's interesting about robotics is they are not just in public spaces. They're in private spaces. They're in semi-private spaces. And so you can link these together in really troubling ways.

Ms. SCHAKOWSKY. Thank you very much.

I yield back.

Mr. BURGESS. Chair thanks the gentlelady. Gentlelady yields back. The Chair recognizes the gentlelady from Indiana, Ms. Brooks, 5 minutes for questions, please.

Ms. BROOKS. Thank you, Mr. Chairman.

I've always really enjoyed the Disrupter Series and pleased to be here to talk about robotics today.

Fortunately, our former mayor of Indianapolis, Mayor Greg Ballard, had the foresight in 2012 to start Indiana State Robotics Initiative to help build that skilled workforce in the pipeline of students, and it is that cross-sector partnership between Government, corporate, and nonprofit organizations to make robotics accessible to all Indiana students.

And I might say, Mr. Kamen, I have visited the Carmel TechHOUNDS. Carmel High School has a FIRST robotics team that's been competing for quite some time. And now, actually, in January, over 160 teams competed in the Indianapolis VEX Robotics Competition.

But throughout Indiana, over 40,000 students are being exposed to robotics and, hopefully, will continue that interest into the future because I do believe that we need to start this exposure very young.

What I am very curious about, Mr. Kamen, is based on all of your experience, what is the one thing you would like us to walk away from in this hearing with respect to how we continue the growth of the FIRST program and of robotics in this country? What is one thing you'd like for us to remember?

Mr. KAMEN. So when I was first asked to come, I thought it would be, hey, let's celebrate, figure out how to grow the robotics program because we know it works, and I was told, Dean, that would be optimistic, you should know that part of this hearing is going to be to deal with real concerns—by the way, some real concerns—but other concerns that some people have that, you know, robots will take jobs. You heard what Mr. Burnstein said and I said. It's hard for me to believe that in the 21st century people will think that advanced technologies are going to do anything except grow this opportunity.

In that regard, I took a slide. I visited Beijing with the president of the U.S. National Academy of Engineers and our chairman for the first-ever coalition meeting of the Royal Society in London, the National Academy, and the Chinese Academy of Engineers, which by the way is way larger than ours.

We get to Beijing to talk about the grand challenges, but I'm whisked away by somebody who takes me to a local school in Beijing. By the way, China, he tells me, has 4,000 FIRST teams.

They use FIRST because it inspires kids to get of the "we are good at learning engineering, but now we learn how to be innovators like you Americans."

And he takes me in there and he shows me this picture on the wall of the president of China. Could you put that slide up? And I asked him, "Will you please tell me why there is a picture of the president of China in this school where I was looking at a FIRST field in Beijing?" And he translated it for me and said, "Robotics will become an entry point, an impetus for growth of the Third Industrial Revolution."

What I want you all to go away understanding is, if America wants to remain a leader in the world economically, in every other way—our security, our economy—it's going to depend on us remaining leaders in the technologies that result from learning how to design and build the next generation of technology, which we generally all call robots now because it's actuators, it's sensors—it's the collection of everything that will allow humans to keep moving.

And if anybody thinks that that's not the case, you're going to be a drag on the future of this country. That's what I think. We need to focus on giving kids the tool sets for the next century, and robotics is a great vehicle to do it.

Ms. BROOKS. Thank you.

Dr. Kota, what would you say are the most significant barriers to investment in advanced robotics? What are the challenges that you are seeing?

Dr. KOTA. Barriers to investment in advanced robotics, you know, we have this national robotics initiative, and actually there is a new solicitation out for a manufacturing innovation institute in robotics, which is all very positive, and I think we should continue to work along the lines of creating next-generation robotics collaborating with humans.

But I don't see any—more than that, I think the biggest barrier—I want to pick up on what Dean Kamen said—the biggest challenge and the biggest opportunity we have right now is really the robots. It is a gateway to engineering.

It is a gateway to designing and building things, and this is the way where we can really get kids excited about going into engineering fields and manufacturing, because that's what it takes to convert an idea into product.

Ms. BROOKS. I agree. But are there barriers that are causing us, that are stopping our—you know, what are the barriers?

Dr. KOTA. Well, are you talking research, or actually educational workforce development?

Ms. BROOKS. Yes.

Dr. KOTA. OK. The workforce development side, the barrier is— OK, the question, I'll turn it around and say we have right now this program is an after-school extracurricular program.

Those kids were already motivated and doing incredible things. We should expose them to every kid in school, and just like we ask every student to dissect a frog, just about, why not ask them to work on these FIRST robotics?

Now, the barrier could potentially be, more than the funding, is actually the requirements for schools to check certain boxes to meet the curriculum requirements.

But there is a way—we know it's working. We can actually map this, what they are doing for FIRST robotics experience, into some of the core curriculum requirements in terms of creative activities in science and math. That's where the barrier is, to actually bringing key stakeholders together and having a discussion.

Ms. BROOKS. Thank you. Thank you.

I yield back.

Mr. BURGESS. The gentlelady yields back. The Chair thanks the gentlelady. Chair recognizes the gentleman from Massachusetts, 5 minutes for your questions, please.

Mr. KENNEDY. Thank you, Chairman.

Thanks again to all the witnesses for coming in and for your testimony earlier.

I know that this hearing isn't about specifically autonomous cars, but autonomous cars are a type of robot that will soon be entering our daily lives and they clearly present some of the ethical issues that come up in the realm of robotics.

Science Magazine recently highlighted a series of surveys to determine consumer attitudes towards autonomous cars.

Their researchers found that survey participants generally support the idea of autonomous cars that might sacrifice passengers to save people outside the vehicle, but they don't actually want to ride in those cars. In other words, people generally choose to save themselves. I'm sure it isn't a huge shock to anybody.

The survey illustrates, though, the so-called trolley problem when faced with two negative scenarios. How do you choose?

So, Dr. Jones, the example of autonomous cars: Without artificial intelligence, a person is going to have to make the decision on how to program the car.

Should it be programmed to protect the passenger at the expense of others? The other way around? How do you make that judgment call? It's a difficult question. But what's happening now with autonomous cars and the types of robots? And if you play out that hypothetical, if you will for me, I'd love to get your guidance on that judgment.

Dr. JONES. I think that right now is the perfect time to answer how we answer that question, which is a great policy problem, and there are two really innovative ideas that I've heard recently. I love the trolley problem. Even a 2-year-old can make a choice about a trolley problem.

There is a YouTube video where he moved all of the people to one side and then runs over all of them. That's one way you could. But the——

Mr. KENNEDY. Which 2-year-old was that exactly?

Dr. JONES. Not my 2-year-old. The other idea is that, why is this a decision that is automatic in every vehicle? The trolley problem asks that individual to look at a moral situation and decide what are your ethics here, and now we say, how do we put this in every single car?

And so Jason Millar argues that that should be a setting. When you get a driverless car, it is your setting just like a trolley problem would be, it is a setting that said, you want to run over the kittens or do you want to, you know, drive off the cliff?

So that is one idea, is to keep autonomy in the hands of the user for ethical questions, which in itself is an ethical design choice.

The other is a Web site called Moral Machines from MIT that is crowdsourcing people's ideas, what they should do, how the car should be designed, not based on the ethics of the engineer but based on what the general public's ideas of ethics are in any given moment, and then those would be embedded into the car.

And so you have less of the ethics of Silicon Valley and the choices of Silicon Valley—and other places, I don't mean to—as sort of a computer—robotics, that's not really true—washing into DC and asking DC to respond to it.

And I think that what these innovative ideas are doing is saying let's all participate in the design and ethical choices that are going into these technologies. And so those are just two alternatives, because there is no right answer to the trolley problem. That's why it's a great—that's why it's a great question.

Mr. KENNEDY. Dr. Kamen?

Mr. KAMEN. I think you can reduce these to philosophical esoteric discussions, which are fun, and maybe there is no perfect answer.

A more basic question might be, in reality this year we'll kill 42,000 people on the highways with drivers that are tweeting or not paying attention or are drunk.

We all know that if a single autonomous vehicle tomorrow hurt or killed somebody, there would be a major national debate about whether there should be another vehicle like that for the foreseeable future.

Yet, every year for decades we kill tens of thousands of people. We hospitalize millions of people. It's the devil we know.

Instead of solving a very esoteric question, you might ask how soon will it be that at least augmented systems would make cars so much safer that, instead of arguing about whether they should be allowed, we should start arguing about whether we should be able to sell vehicles that don't have these systems. Because we know how many people we are killing all the time.

Mr. KENNEDY. And at the risk of getting into that philosophical debate, I would agree with you that we say, let's move forward because, look, if we can reduce that from 42,000 to one, obviously, that's an extraordinary—or to zero or to whatever it is, to less than 42,000—that's an extraordinary innovation, and we want to incentivize that.

The question, basically, and perhaps you can say a little bit of expertise in the seven seconds I'll give you, but if it comes down to essentially an algorithm of saying if-then, right, in a complex if-then decision tree for a computer code, that is then scaled up across every single car, that is a choice that somebody's got to make.

So I'm not, you know, asking so much what that right decision is but what's the right way for evaluating how we make those decisions, understanding that, if we can make progress on this, that's tremendous and we don't want to stop that innovation. But it does bring up ethical issues that we haven't had to confront in this scenario before.

Mr. KAMEN. And I guess all I would say is those are fantastic debates to have and, as we all know, the good is the enemy of the great.

I guess what I would come back to say, however, is we should discuss those issues and what the available technologies are in the context of the real alternatives and we should be accelerating the use of these technologies that overall will hugely reduce injuries and deaths because these technologies don't get distracted.

Inevitably, as we said before, every powerful technology can have mischievous and nefarious users. Every powerful technology will eventually show a weakness or need to be improved.

But the day we start saying, because of those issues we will slow down or stop progress, is the day we are in big trouble.

Mr. BURGESS. Gentleman yields back. Chair thanks the gentleman.

I believe we are going to have time for a second round, if anyone wishes to stay. When we initiate that then, Mr. Kamen, I'm going to stay with you on that same concept.

And we had a tragic accident in our district with a distracted driving situation where four women—two in one car, two in the other—head-on collision, they all died.

And so lane departure warning device that—you know, you're right. You almost had—there should be like anti-lock brakes. There should be, like, a supplemental restraint device or an airbag or a seatbelt.

It almost should be standard equipment, especially in the day and age where we all have a device that could potentially distract us while we are driving.

So I think that is a powerful concept and one which, of course, in this subcommittee we'll continue to explore because we have the National Highway Traffic Safety Administration under our jurisdiction.

So I appreciate your comments there. Just more broadly, and you now have touched upon something that I kind of debated whether or not I should bring up. But just let's talk—we have got a panel of experts.

I mean, we live under the tyranny of Federal agencies—at least, that's my opinion. Mr. Kennedy may disagree. Federal Trade Commission, Consumer Product Safety Commission, National Highway Traffic Safety Administration is just this subcommittee's jurisdiction.

But there is also the Department of Labor, Health and Human Services, Department of Energy, Department of Education, Department of Energy—I'm sorry, Department of Commerce. I almost had a Rick Perry moment there for a minute. Department of Commerce. So how do you see the intersection of all these Federal agencies, and they don't make anything neat or cool like you all do. They write regulations, to regulate the neat and cool stuff that you all do.

I know it's a big discussion, but as briefly as you can, could you just kind of give us some sense of the direction of how the regulatory environment should proceed in this very new area?

Mr. Kamen, we will start with you and just work down the table, if you would.

Mr. KAMEN. Well, I can give you one very relevant to the self-driving car, I think, because you have a regulatory agency, NHTSA, and you have one called the FAA. And there is a lesson here.

When I learned to fly, you had simple autopilots. They weren't very good and they could get you wings—they could do a few simple things.

But you were very clearly told when you go take your flight test, you many not turn that on. It was a crutch. They want to make sure you could really fly that plane. You're not allowed to use it.

Over the decades, as those things got better, they started requiring them in their sophisticated aircraft because when you're doing mach-point-8 and you're coming in to a very low ceiling, no human is as good as that autopilot, and then they went to allowing you to use it, then testing you on how you use it.

Then they made it part of what's called the MEL, the minimal equipment list: You are not allowed to fly this airplane under these conditions unless that thing is working and is on.

I think we shifted. The FAA has demonstrated, we went from people have to fly to it's not safe unless that thing is working and you legally can't do it and you wouldn't want to get on an airliner traveling around this country if that autopilot on minimum condi-

55

tions that was going to land coming out that fog and touching down two seconds later. It's not legal to do it. It's not safe to do it.

I think, certainly, in your lifetime, the question is going to be with somebody sitting up there, Should we allow people to drive cars? I know they think it's fun, but this is so dangerous that allowing them that privilege of running around at 60 miles an hour with a 3,000-pound machine and we can't be sure they are not drunk and tired, I'm not sure we should allow that anymore.

That's why we have autopilots, and you're going to see that change happen. But human understanding always lags the rate at which technical opportunities arise, and it's always the next generation that adopts it.

You know, what was indefensible to your parents was indispensable to you, and what your kids will think of as normal you will be concerned about. Technology really is anything that wasn't available when you were a kid.

But I think NHTSA should take a lesson from FAA. They both regulate critical activities, but as we see technology developing, we know there are loopholes.

We know there are disasters. We know things can go wrong. But that shouldn't present an alternative that we don't aggressively go after improving.

Mr. BURGESS. Very well. Dr. Kota.

Dr. KOTA. A different context—I was making a similar statement about how FDA could potentially take some ideas from FAA.

I have had a little bit of experience working on aircraft designs, and what I was surprised to note is that—which many of you probably know already—if you are designing any new component or system, what are released for an aircraft, there are a clear set of guidelines and regulations for what's safe and what's not—and, by the way, NHTSA, FDA, FAA, they all care about safety. I'm glad they do.

But the way the FAA works—Dean, you probably know DERs— they have experts who are authorized——

Mr. KAMEN. DER is designated engineering representative.

Dr. KOTA. Designated engineering—yes. DER is for FAA. So if you are a small business or a large business, they work with you to make sure you are following the proper regulations so you are not spending three years designing, building and going and finding out that, oh, the FAA doesn't accept it.

These regulations are meant for the right reasons and also they actually help accelerate innovation, if they do it right. So on that note, if similar DERs we can have not only with NHTSA but also with even FDA and others, too, I think that's a very good practice.

Mr. BURGESS. I'm going to suspend that question temporarily and go back to Mr. Kennedy for 5 minutes for questions, please.

Mr. KENNEDY. I'm happy to yield you another 3 minutes if you want.

Mr. BURGESS. Very well. We'll continue on the regulatory environment going forward.

Dr. Jones.

Mr. KENNEDY. I'd just like the record to reflect that he said that regulation accelerates innovation. So there you go.

Mr. BURGESS. I wish it could. I was asking the panel.

Dr. JONES. I can repeat it, if that's helpful.

I think that it is important to remember that, like Mr. Kamen said, when we talk about robotics AI, we are talking about technology. It's just a really broad term and so the ethical issues with drones are not the same ethical issues as with driverless cars.

So it would be very hard to sit down and say, How do we solve all of the ethical problems with robotics with using the same mechanism?

And so I think inevitably these technological advancements occur within sectors.

Mr. BURGESS. I will interrupt you just for a moment because so many times at the Federal agency level it is putting the square peg in a round hole. I mean, that's what they do.

Dr. JONES. So the FAA handling drones and the transportation people handling driverless cars causes lots of problems and I was at a Department of Homeland Security roundtable, I guess you would call it, that was also sponsored by NSF, and what it did was brought these people together and we realized that, OK, a lot of these drone problems are not the same problems as the driverless cars, and that's fine.

But there were some shared problems and there was some policy innovation that was happening in the driverless car that had not occurred in the drone area.

And so I think that there were huge benefits to bringing everyone to the table, and I think that a great role for the Federal Government is saying, you guys have to keep talking to each other, you have to keep coming to the table. We don't want redundancies that I think can occur across agencies.

And this was a two-day event where vocabulary was shared that we realized we were talking over each other and using different words for the same things. And so it was a great use of time, and I think that a really simple what can we do—it just continued to create these deliberative spaces.

Mr. BURGESS. Mr. Burnstein, either your thoughts or your association's thoughts on the regulatory environment going forward and its ability to facilitate or impede development.

Mr. BURNSTEIN. Well, in preparation for this hearing, I talked to some of our members about that, and they don't see regulatory issues as a major problem in preventing them from advancing robotics.

They did talk about some of the issues related to safety. So our association developed the American National Robot Safety Standard, and when you got to this area of collaborative robots, right, so the OSHA inspectors knew about when the robot was behind a fence how to treat that.

But now we have these collaborative robot installations that are there, and it's different from region to region, and it's also different from country to country.

And so our members are saying, look, we set up a safe application here in the U.S., but then when we go to Canada we got to deal with changing it to meet another safety regulation.

Is there some way that these international applications that are safe in one country can be seen as safe in the others? Is there something the Government can do on that?

But that's as far as it went in terms of the regulatory discussion.

Mr. BURGESS. Very well.

The Chair recognizes the gentleman from Massachusetts, 5 minutes for questions, please.

Mr. KENNEDY. Thank you, Mr. Chairman.

Just keep it, if I can, to 30 seconds for each of you. Given that the issues that you underscored in your testimony and the questions, 30 seconds each.

What recommendations would you give to Congress as we try to balance these issues and Incentivize the innovation going forward? What should we be thinking about? What should we be talking about, and what should we do and what shouldn't we do? Thirty seconds. Dr. Kamen.

Mr. KAMEN. If you wanted the answer related to regulation, I think any rational person realizes well-established regulations that allow people to interact consistently—there would be no Internet.

Clearly, a regulatory environment can be hugely useful. Unfortunately, the time it takes to get clarity and get some of these regulations in place as technology is moving faster and faster is making the time difference between when the thing is possible to when the regulation has clarity is slowing things down, and there is a natural incentive of business to move faster and faster and there is a natural incentive of regulators to be more and more conservative and concerned, and that gap is getting so large that it's slowing down access to medical miracles.

It's slowing down opportunities. So I would urge you to find a way to make sure that all the regulators are highly incentivized to do things quickly, even if it's incrementally, to do it quickly and do it with certainty.

Mr. KENNEDY. Thank you.

Dr. Kota.

Dr. KOTA. Again, sir, well said. I'd just add one more point. Just going back to things like DER is what FAA does. Let's find analogous components in other NHTSA and FDA and what have you, from a regulation point of view.

One more thing I want to add is that the strategic and coordinated investment by the Federal Government, not each agency running in different directions, if you want true innovation we need to connect the dots.

So the best ideas coming at a national science forum, from NASA and the Department of Defense, you know, leveraging the procurement capability of the Department of Defense.

So these are the things we can connect the dots and accelerate innovation, including regulation. That's one important thing I want to suggest.

Mr. KENNEDY. Thank you.

Dr. Jones.

Dr. JONES. I would suggest that the balance of pros and cons is adjusted. I think that people are left out when technology advances and often the policies that we put choose. We just say, "Here are the pros, here are the cons. The pros outweigh the cons, and so we are making this choice." But instead to embrace the cons as part of the policy solution itself, and I think we've heard a lot about not just job displacement today but also what do we do with the displaced.

That's all part, I think, of the same policy. Not a choice to say, well, these factories have these benefits but to make sure that people who don't design and don't have these technologies are also part of the policy equation.

Mr. KENNEDY. Thank you.

Mr. BURNSTEIN. I would say continue to support the National Robotics Initiative. That has a major impact around the world in drawing attention to the importance of robotics.

And in the U.S. I think that stimulated innovation. I think that we need to continue establishing centers that get the technology that's being developed in the U.S. into the hands of small and medium-sized companies.

We have some mechanism in place now. I think we could do more, and I think the training issue is very important. We have to prepare the workforce for the jobs of the future and, as I said, the jobs today.

The number-one challenge our members face: They can't fill all the jobs that they have open today.

Mr. KENNEDY. Thank you.

Mr. BURGESS. Gentleman yields back.

Seeing that there are no further Members wishing to ask questions from this panel, I do want to thank our witnesses for being here today. It's been a very good and lively discussion, and I look forward to further discussions on this in the future.

So, pursuant to committee rules, I will remind Members they have 10 business days to submit additional questions for the record, and I ask the witnesses to submit their response to those questions within 10 business days upon receipt of the questions.

Without objection, then, the subcommittee is adjourned.

[Whereupon, at 11:55 a.m., the subcommittee was adjourned.]